Bumble
the Brave Kitten
and other true stories about fantastic felines

Sam Hay

CATS
PROTECTION

MACMILLAN CHILDREN'S BOOKS

First published 2010 by Macmillan Children's Books
a division of Macmillan Publishers Limited
20 New Wharf Road, London N1 9RR
Basingstoke and Oxford
Associated companies throughout the world
www.panmacmillan.com

ISBN 978-0-330-52181-9

A CIP catalogue record for this book is available from
the British Library.

Typeset by Ellipsis Books Limited, Glasgow
Printed and bound in the UK by CPI Mackays, Chatham ME5 8TD

Contents

Tizer

It was the end of another hectic day at King's Cross Police Station. Inspector Roy Sloane stretched out his legs and sighed. His desk groaned under files – reports of bag snatchers, lost brief-cases, missing wallets, vandals. It was all in a day's work for the police team based at one of the busiest railway stations in the country.

He leaned back in his chair and rubbed his screen-weary eyes. And that was when he felt it – a slight tickle around his left ankle, followed swiftly by another to his right. He glanced down and shuddered. 'Mice!' he growled, as two dark shadows shot out from beneath his desk and disappeared behind a filing cabinet.

Bumble the Brave Kitten

They were everywhere – scuttling behind the skirting boards and lurking in dark corners. The canteen was teeming with them. A large colony had moved in months ago and at times it felt like every mouse in London was currently 'bed & breakfasting' at King's Cross Police Station.

Inspector Sloane picked up the phone and dialled a familiar number.

'Is that Pest Control?' he said. 'This is Inspector Sloane at King's Cross again. You need to send someone down here – our mouse problem is worse than ever!'

The voice at the other end sounded weary. 'Is the poison that we put down still not working?'

'Nope, not at all,' said the Inspector, catching sight of another little black shape, lurking behind the bin in the corner of the room. 'They're everywhere!'

'OK, I'll send someone down to lay more poison,' said the voice with a sigh.

'But the poison isn't working!' said the Inspector, quietly slipping off one of his boots, and taking aim. 'I've got more mice down here than passengers!' He heaved the boot at the bin, and the dark shadow darted away under a cupboard.

'Perhaps you should get yourself a cat then,' said the voice with a chuckle.

Inspector Sloane sat up. 'Yes,' he said. 'Maybe I should.'

'What?' said the voice on the phone. 'I was only joking; a cat won't work.'

'Well, it can't be any worse than you lot,' said the Inspector. 'And it'll cost me a lot less. In fact, don't bother coming down, I'll get a cat instead.'

'What? Hello? . . . Hello?'

But Inspector Sloane had already hung up. He retrieved his boot and put on his hat. It was time to find a new recruit for his force.

★

Bumble the Brave Kitten

'So what sort of cat are you looking for, Inspector?'

Roy Sloane shrugged. 'Any sort, so long as it can catch a mouse!'

Alex grinned. She'd been working at the Cats Protection's North London Adoption Centre for years, and she'd matched many a lost cat with a new owner.

'Have a look around and see if there's one that catches your eye – though I usually find that a cat will pick you.'

Inspector Sloane was not a cat man. He preferred dogs. But he had little time for either with a busy station to run, and a lively family at home. He glanced around him. On either side of him were glass pens, each containing one, or sometimes two, lost-looking cats. Some were pitiful: thin and scrawny, with chewed ears, and mangled tails, others were big and chunky – all lost pets, waiting and hoping to be reclaimed or rehomed. Most turned to greet him, rubbing their heads or paws against the glass, meowing, yowling.

Inspector Sloane walked on, not knowing how to choose. And then he saw him. The only one *not* trying to attract his attention: a stocky white and tabby tom, with his back to the glass, his head turned to the wall, staring blankly at nothing.

'What's wrong with him?'

Alex sighed. 'Poor Tizer. He was an old lady's lap-cat. But she died, and he ended up here. He's taken it badly.'

For no reason whatsoever, Inspector Sloane felt drawn to the cat. He peered in at the pen, but the cat continued to ignore him.

'It's been hard finding him a home,' admitted Alex. 'He's got a lovely nature, but he's quite old – almost fifteen, and most people don't want an old cat. Loads of people have passed him by; I think he's given up trying to find a new owner.'

It had never occurred to the Inspector that cats

could feel abandoned, unwanted and ignored. Nor had he realized that people might pass by an older cat, just because they felt he was too ancient to bother with.

'Does he play?' he asked gruffly.

Alex nodded. 'He's got a toy spider tucked under his paws. If you look closely you can see it. He loves it – if you throw it for him, he'll bring it back to you.'

'Just like a dog,' chuckled the Inspector softly. 'I'll have him,' he said, in a firm voice that surprised even him. Instinctively he knew *this* was the cat he should have. Police Constable Tizer was hired.

Of course the Inspector couldn't just scoop him up and take him there and then. There were forms to fill, checks to be made. The Cats Protection Adoption Centre staff had to be certain Tizer was going somewhere suitable.

Tizer

Home checks were essential — even if that new home was a police station! Tizer was an indoor cat — he'd spent all his life in a small flat in a tower block. And he would stay indoors at the police station, safe from the busy roads and railways outside — but with more space to explore than he'd ever had before.

A week later, Inspector Sloane retraced his steps, this time with a pet carrier, ready to collect Tizer.

'Don't worry if he's a bit shy at first,' said Alex, as she led the Inspector back down the same aisle of pens. 'It can take them a while to settle in.'

Tizer was in the same position as last time — with his back to the glass. When Alex opened his pen, he showed no interest. He was used to people coming and going, and passing by.

'Come on, lad,' said the Inspector gently. 'Let's go home.'

The offices of the British Transport Police

stand to the side of King's Cross Station. Millions of people pass along its platforms each year, many commuting to work.

It was rush hour on a Monday morning when Tizer first got a glimpse of his new home. It didn't look promising: busy streets, heavy traffic, noise, smells and city chaos. For a cat that had spent all his life in one little old lady's living room, King's Cross Station was a shock. But he needn't have worried. A few moments later, they stepped out of the hustle and bustle of the railway station into the police building, and Tizer's new life officially began.

That first night was an experience neither Tizer nor the Inspector would ever forget.

Roy Sloane had brought his sleeping bag – he was planning to bed down in his office, and stay near Tizer in case the cat was afraid. But neither cat nor man got much sleep that night. Every time the Inspector got comfy, Tizer would climb on top of him and sit on his head, or chase his toes through the sleeping bag, or just walk up and down him, snuffling and butting him with his head.

But by the morning a bond had been made. Tizer had 'chosen' the Inspector. From that night on, he would never stray far from the Inspector's side. And the Inspector, a life-long dog lover who had always shied away from cats, had taken the scrawny old tom cat very much to his heart.

'He caught one!' A grinning constable proudly held up a small black rodent: Tizer's first trophy.

He'd been in the station for two weeks, and had settled in quickly. There had been a few small wobbles. He was scared of the sirens that alerted the staff to an emergency call-out, and it had taken him a day or two to adjust to the hustle and bustle of the police station. But he adapted fast, and soon discovered warm corners, where he could nap undisturbed for hours. He also found the 'station softies', who'd keep cat treats in their drawers, and always had a warm lap on offer. He knew where to find people to play with him – people ready to throw his spider, or give him a belly tickle. But in between treats and tickles, he had also found time to do his duty . . .

Inspector Sloane grinned. 'That's the first mouse I've seen since Tizer got here. I reckon the rest have scarpered!'

It was true. Since Tizer's arrival, not a single mouse had been seen. The plan had worked.

Inspector Sloane bent down and picked up the cat, already purring and butting his hand for a stroke. He rubbed his ears, and stroked his head . . . But just then, there was a shout.

'Inspector!' One of the constables was beckoning him over. He put down the cat and nodded to the young constable. 'What's the problem?'

Tizer

'We've got a young lad in the interview room, sir. He's run away from home after a row with his mum. He's been sleeping rough for a few nights. He's in a bit of a state, but he won't say what his name is, or where he's from. He's very young.'

Inspector Sloane knocked gently on the door, and went in.

The boy was sitting at the table, a blanket wrapped round his shoulders, a can of Coke untouched in front of him. His hair hung damply against his head and his face was dirty. There were tear stains on his cheeks.

'My name is Inspector Roy Sloane,' the Inspector said gently. 'Could you tell me your name?'

The boy looked down at his hands, but said nothing.

'Don't worry, lad,' said the Inspector. 'You're not in any trouble, but we can't help you unless you tell us your name and where you're from.'

Again nothing.

Just then, the door opened and another constable came in, carrying a pile of files. Tizer padded in behind her, and headed straight for the boy. He sat purring at his feet, gently butting his ankles and calves, looking for a stroke. Inspector Sloane stood up, about to put the cat out, when the boy stirred, and slowly reached down to stroke him. After a few moments, Tizer jumped up, on to the boy's lap, nuzzling and purring loudly. For a moment or two no one moved, and then the boy started to cry softly. He bent down and cuddled Tizer closer, burying his face in the cat's soft fur. 'My name is Joe,' he whispered. 'I'm ten. I want to go home.'

PC Tizer stayed with Joe until his mum came to collect him a few hours later.

Days turned into weeks, and weeks to months, and Tizer become more than just the police station mouser; he was family – one of the team. He became skilled at calming and helping kids who visited the station: runaways, lost children, kids who had fallen in with the wrong crowd, shop-lifters, vandals . . . No one asked Tizer to get involved, he just did. Somehow he was able to sense when someone was sad and needed a cuddle, or just a distraction from whatever unhappiness had brought them to the station.

And it wasn't just kids. The police officers turned to him too. After a stressful call-out, many would seek out Tizer. A few games of throw-the-spider, or just a cuddle and a stroke were enough to calm and console. Officers learned to type one-handed, so they could cuddle him while they worked. Tizer was making his mark, in lots of ways – you could spot a King's Cross bobby straight away from the white fluff all over their black uniforms!

Tizer had the run of the station and was a

regular in the interview room, though he had to be ejected a few times when his purring drowned out an offender's confession on the interview tapes.

He had his own chair in the meeting room – and his own table in the mess room, where he developed a taste for chilli kebabs with the officers working the nightshift. But generally his needs were simple. With the few teeth he had left, he liked his food soft, and at night he liked to bed down in Inspector Sloane's office – tucked up in a small cardboard box, under his desk.

But at nearly fifteen he was starting to show his age. He was a messy eater, and his face and fur were always dirty. One Friday evening, Inspector Sloane gathered him up and decided to take him home with him to the country for a few days. He booked a 'pet groomer' to come round and sort him out: cut his nails and give him a wash.

But Inspector Sloane's plans of a brief weekend

visit were scuppered the first night that he and Tizer arrived home.

'Dad!' The Inspector's eight-year-old son Jake flew out of the house to greet him – and then did a double take. 'You brought him home?'

Jake had heard tales of Tizer, of course, but had never imagined he'd actually meet him. He scooped the cat up in his arms, and fussed over him as only a kid can do. Tizer wasn't fazed. It was mutual love at first sight. He purred and snuggled. And when bedtime came, he followed Jake and his older brother Ben straight upstairs, and settled down for the night on one of their beds. It was as though he'd lived there all his life.

When Monday came, and it was time for Tizer to leave, Jake was devastated. 'You can't take him back, Dad. I love him.'

And deep down, Inspector Sloane knew that Jake was right. He couldn't take him back. Tizer had been on an incredible journey. He'd gone from quiet old lap-cat to PC Tizer, dealing with hundreds of people every day, in one of the busiest police stations in the country. He'd sorted out the mouse problem and boosted morale among the station's staff. He'd calmed and consoled kids, and brought joy and happiness to many people. But he was tired now. He deserved a rest.

So Tizer retired to the country, and after almost fifteen years of being an indoor cat, he discovered the joys of outdoor life. But just like any retired police officer, he was never really off-duty. He made a daily patrol of his garden, taking up a post on the fence where he could spot intruders and keep order. And when a sparrow hawk (a bird of prey the same size as himself) dared to land in his garden, he not only caught it – but also the sparrow it was trying to catch. He proudly took both inside to show Mrs Sloane, and couldn't quite understand why she wasn't nearly as chuffed with his 'arrests', as the officers at Kings Cross had been when he caught his first mouse.

Both birds escaped unhurt, and from then on Tizer contented himself with hunting for sausages at family barbecues instead.

Tizer relished his retirement and was spoilt rotten by his family. There was only one thing he could never get used to – Inspector Sloane's bagpipes! A keen piper, Inspector Sloane soon found himself banished to a back bedroom when he needed to practise, so that PC Tizer could get on with enjoying his well-deserved rest and relaxation!

Stewie

It was a damp Saturday afternoon in November. Kevan was face down in the mud, his clothes soaking wet, trying his best to scramble under a huge army net. For a brief second he wondered what on earth he was doing. What had possessed him to sign up for such madness? Then he thought of Stewie, and he gritted his teeth. Head down, he crawled even faster.

The contest was called *The Survival of the Fittest* and it certainly lived up to its name. Competitors had to run, swim and climb their way through a 12 km army-style assault course as fast as they could. Kevan and his colleague Debbie were both taking part, helping each other to complete the course. At forty-eight, Kevan was no teenager, but he was in good shape; much better than some. All around him men and women were puffing and panting and cursing their way through the course, while the soldiers supervising the event bawled at them loudly, to make sure they got the authentic 'army' experience!

Kevan was halfway there now. He'd already made it over the three-metre-high hay bales, and swum the river – twice. He'd been through the builders' yard and the urban jungle – squeezing down pipes, and hauling himself over tyres and oil drums. Even the monkey bars hadn't defeated him, though many of the much younger 'muscle men' had struggled with that bit.

Kevan knew he could do this. He was a fighter, just like Stewie. So he ignored the aches and pains, the blisters on blisters, and the chaffing from his river-soaked clothes, and concentrated instead on getting through. If he did, he'd raise a bundle of cash for Stewie – a tiny bedraggled little kitten who'd come into his life just a few weeks ago.

Stewie appeared one afternoon in October. The Cats Protection Adoption Centre in Nottingham was busy, as always. Kevan was on duty, taking calls about cats, guiding potential adopters to the right pet, and signing in the new arrivals; cats who through no fault of their own had suddenly found themselves homeless. Cats just like Stewie.

Kevan had seen the man with the cardboard box arrive. He had a sheepish look about him.

'Can I help you?'

The man swallowed hard. He looked uncomfortable. 'I found this cat and kittens in my garden,' he said, not looking Kevan in the eye. 'They're not mine!' he added, still not looking at Kevan. 'The cat's been hanging around for a while now, then when I saw it had kittens, I thought

I'd best bring them in . . .' He trailed off, waiting for Kevan to encourage him, reward him even, for his community spirit and, more importantly, for Kevan to accept the box.

'Let's have a look then,' sighed Kevan, ignoring the slight bubble of apprehension in his belly. He always felt it when faced with a box. The trouble was, you never knew what awful story you might find inside. And after seventeen years at the Adoption Centre, Kevan had seen some terrible things.

He carefully opened the lid, talking softly, so as not to scare the animals inside.

There were four kittens, nestled close to their mum. She looked out anxiously, though not aggressively. That was the first flaw in the man's story — *if* the cat had really been a wandering stray, Kevan would have expected her to be more hostile, especially with her kittens to protect. But she wasn't. She was obviously used to being handled, petted even. So were her kittens. She let

Kevan stroke her gently, and didn't mind when he scooped up one of the tiny bundles to examine it. He grimaced. The kitten was riddled with fleas. They all were.

'I think they're about seven or eight weeks old,' said the man, feeling more confident now.

But Kevan wasn't listening. He was carefully looking over the rest of the litter, his professional eye falling on the smallest one, a black and white kitten that had been pushed out to the side. It didn't respond much to his careful prodding and checking. It was lethargic, barely mewing, its eyes flicking open, then shut. He could tell at once it was ill. Gravely so.

'Fleas,' said Kevan, shaking his head. He'd seen bad infestations before, of course. But this was one of the worst. The fleas looked just like tiny black pinpricks, covering the roots of the fur. Most cats got the odd one or two but, left untreated, they spread quickly, laying thousands of eggs, until colonies of them would literally suck the lifeblood out of the cat. Such cases were often fatal for kittens. Kevan knew if this litter were to survive they'd need urgent medical treatment. Though, by the looks of it, it was already too late for the smallest one.

As soon as the man had gone, Kevan took them to the vet. The mum cat and the rest of the litter would be fine, but the smallest one, whom they'd named Stewie, was in a very bad way. He would need round-the-clock care. It would be expensive, but Cats Protection didn't put a price on the life of any cat or kitten. They always did as much as they could – giving each one a fighting chance. This little kitten was certainly fighting. Fighting for his life.

Stewie lay now in an intensive care pen, a drip attached to his tiny body, his eyes closed.

'Come on!' said Kevan softly. 'Stay with us.'

Bumble the Brave Kitten

He stroked the tiny black head gently with one finger, while a nurse listened to the kitten's heart-beat. It was very weak.

Stewie was suffering from advanced anaemia; the fleas had sucked so much blood out of him that he didn't have enough red blood cells to function properly. He was tiny, weak and severely dehydrated. The drip was giving him much needed fluid, but he was still dangerously ill. He'd already crashed several times since he'd arrived at the vet's; his heart had literally stopped beating . . . but each time, they'd managed to bring him back. He was still alive, but barely.

'Come on! Keep fighting, Stewie,' Kevan said again. This time, at the sound of his voice, Stewie opened his eyes, and took a small breath, followed, after a pause, by another. Somehow he was still clinging on.

The nurse listened again to his heartbeat. 'For such a little scrap, he has a strong will to live,' she said. Kevan nodded. He'd seen many brave cats in his time. But there was something special about Stewie.

Later, Kevan returned to the Adoption Centre. He knew that if Stewie made it through the night, he might have a chance. But it didn't look likely.

As the sun rose the next morning, Stewie surprised them all. Somehow he still clung on. The vet and the nurse were both shocked that he'd survived the night. Several times they'd even considered putting Stewie to sleep, to spare him any more suffering. But each time they'd fetched the needle, the little kitten had suddenly rallied, almost as though he was trying to tell them not to give up on him.

'I want to try something different now,' said the vet when she called Kevan that morning. 'He desperately needs more blood – I think we should attempt a blood transfusion from his mum.'

It was a treatment that had been used to treat anaemia in humans for years. It was becoming much more commonplace in veterinary medicine too – but Stewie was so ill, there was no guarantee it would make much difference. And his mum, who was the most suitable donor, was thin and run-down herself. But the vet wanted to try. She'd been touched by the little kitten's battle to survive, and felt he deserved a chance.

And her efforts were rewarded. A few hours later, the signs were good. The transfusion seemed to have given Stewie the boost he needed. He was still sleeping, but more peacefully now. And by the third day, he was awake, and alert enough for Sam, one of Kevan's colleagues at the Adoption Centre, to take him home with him for the night. But Sam barely made it home before the kitten collapsed again. Sam turned round and took him straight back to the vet's.

The kitten appeared to be fading fast, and there wasn't much more the vet could do. The nurse offered to take Stewie home with her. She had the knowledge and experience to care for him, but it would be a difficult night.

When Stewie woke up on the fourth day, he was unusually alert. He still looked very poorly – the tips of his black fur had actually turned grey overnight with the shock of his illness. But his huge eyes had lost their glassy stare, and in its place was a slight light, a twinkle even. Somehow Stewie had battled his demons, and won.

'Gentle now, Ruby . . . He's very small . . .'

Kevan's enormous lurcher dog had a soft spot for cats. Kevan often brought them home; abandoned newborn kittens, needing to be bottle-fed, or sickly cats that needed extra care. Now it was Stewie's turn. Kevan had collected him from the vet's and brought him home for a week. Ruby was delighted! Kevan and his family already had four cats of their own – all rescue cats, and the dog adored them. She even forgave their bad behaviour; they ruled Ruby mercilessly, bossing her around, jumping on her, taking her toys, stealing her treats . . . but she didn't care.

The sight of little Stewie, a tiny black and white fluffball, small enough to fit in Kevan's shoe, had the lurcher overwhelmed with joy. Most cats would be alarmed at the sight of such a large, boisterous dog, but Stewie was so weak that there could have been a living room full of wolves and he wouldn't have noticed. He certainly wasn't in any danger from Ruby. She was a big daft dog with a huge heart and a very sweet nature. She also had a special gentleness, often found in only the biggest of dogs.

'Come on then, Ruby,' said Kevan, smiling. 'Come and say hello to Stewie.' The dog trotted over delightedly, nuzzling the kitten kindly, giving him a comforting lick or two. She could tell instinctively how poorly he was, and was even more careful than usual. Afterwards, she settled down at Kevan's feet, on duty, ready to help in any way she could.

Caring for Stewie was an intensive job. He was so weak he needed to be syringe-fed with liquid food for the first few days, but as his strength returned Kevan eventually persuaded him to eat proper food again, and his recovery speeded up as a result. Ruby, meanwhile, stayed close, keeping a motherly eye on the kitten. By the end of the week, the pair had become firm friends. Kevan would often find them cuddled up together, the tiny kitten sitting between Ruby's enormous paws. He was a cheeky little lad. And he would often get up on his back legs and playfully bat the big dog on the chops. Ruby loved it, wagging her tail delightedly.

Stewie's spirit seemed to touch everyone. He

was now a wide-eyed ball of mischief, full of fun and high spirits. But caring for the kitten had been expensive. A few days later, when the bill arrived for Stewie's medical treatment, Kevan realized it was time for action. While the kitten continued to grow stronger and healthier under his care, Kevan dug out his running shoes. He and his colleague Debbie had found a sure-fire way to raise some much-needed cash to pay for the treatment Stewie had received – they signed up for a sponsored army-style assault course . . . *The Survival of the Fittest!*

'*COME ON THEN! LET'S BE HAVING YOU!*'

Kevan gritted his teeth. He'd made it through the mud, scrambling and crawling as fast as he could, until he reached the end of the net. He'd already beaten the rope swing and conquered another set of monkey bars. He'd hauled himself up slippery scaffolding. He'd clambered through a jungle of wrecked cars and truck tyres. He'd found his way through a metal maze, and now, finally, he'd reached the last hurdle of the course: the great wall! It loomed menacingly in front of him; a sheer, solid barrier, eight feet tall. Kevan stopped for a second, to catch his breath and have a good look at it. He ached all over, he was soaked to the skin, and he was utterly exhausted. And now this! The final obstacle, the toughest of all, came just when every one of his muscles was screaming at him to stop. Then he grinned, and thought of that tiny little black and white scrap, the fur of his coat turning grey with the stress he'd endured. He thought about the way he'd clung to life, never giving up, bravely beating the odds. If Stewie could do it, so could Kev. With one final burst of energy, he threw himself at the wall, and was up and over in seconds. He'd done it. Done it for Stewie!

Bumble the Brave Kitten

The event raised hundreds of pounds for Stewie's fund. But Kevan and Debbie weren't done yet. They started to plan more fundraisers: marathons and bike rides . . . And their colleague Vicki came up with an even more daring idea. She planned to spend two days locked inside a cat pen, in a bid to raise yet more money for Stewie.

The kitten, meanwhile, was growing stronger and healthier by the day. And Kevan realized it was time for him to find a home of his own. It was difficult. Kevan had grown very fond of the kitten – but he couldn't keep him. His house was already bursting at the seams with Ruby and the cats!

As soon as Stewie was well enough, Kevan returned him to the Adoption Centre, where he made himself straight at home. He followed the staff around, sitting on their shoulders while they worked, clambering over their keyboards and generally getting into everything – just as a kitten should. He was eating well, and sleeping well. And although he was still small for his age, he was gradually catching up.

Then one afternoon a family phoned. They were looking for a kitten. They asked if they could visit the centre . . .

'That's them!' said Kevan, nudging Debbie as, a few days later, the family approached the reception desk. 'They're the ones for Stewie!'

Debbie smiled. Kevan always got a gut feeling about people – and he knew immediately that he liked this family. And the more he spoke to them, and the more he found out about them, the more he trusted them. They were the right family for Stewie.

The Gregory family had been thinking about getting a cat for a while. Their son Jacob, who was eight, talked about little else. And their three-year-old daughter Ruby loved all things fluffy. Ruby! The little girl even had the same name as Kevan's big-hearted lurcher who adored Stewie – a small coincidence, but it felt like another sign that this was a perfect match. And it was.

From the day Stewie went home with the Gregorys he fitted in like one of the family. Some kittens might have been fazed by family life. But not Stewie – he took to the Gregorys immediately. He loved the kids – quickly becoming Jacob's little shadow, endlessly playing with the lad, and happily snuggling up to him for a cuddle. And even little Ruby – an energetic bundle of fun herself – didn't worry Stewie. A few days after his arrival, Ruby's parents popped their heads around the living-room door to find Stewie playing dolls' tea parties, with a plate, fake cake and a cup of tea all to himself! After spending so much time with people at the vet's and at the Adoption Centre, Stewie enjoyed human company. And he thrived on the love and attention he got at the Gregorys'. Even the tiny grey hairs on his coat, for so long a symbol of the stress and suffering he'd been through, suddenly and unexpectedly started to disappear. The little battler had fought hard, and won.

Speedy

Joan had been worried for weeks.

'We have got to do *something*,' she said to her husband as they got ready for bed one chilly November night. 'Christine just isn't herself. I can feel her unhappiness all around her.'

David had felt it too. Christine, their nineteen-year-old daughter, was severely disabled, and as a result led a quiet, isolated and often lonely life. She suffered from a number of difficult conditions – leaving her unable to walk, talk or even move freely.

She lived with her parents and her younger brother – also called David, after his father, and tragically affected by the same cruel genetic condition as his sister. Both children were loved and cherished by their devoted parents, but Joan sensed that for Christine, this wasn't enough any more.

'She needs something of her own,' she said softly to herself, as she turned off the bedside light. 'Something to bring a little sunshine into her life.'

David squeezed her hand in the darkness. 'We'll think of something,' he said gently.

The idea came to her that night. Joan wasn't sure if she'd dreamed it. But by morning, she knew what to do. She thought about it as she gently washed Christine and her brother, dressed them and made breakfast. She chatted away cheerfully, as she always did, but the idea was growing stronger in her mind, and the more she looked at Christine, the more certain she became.

Christine had endured much in her young life.

She was often confined to bed, frequently in pain, and suffered regular epileptic fits. As the years passed, her condition worsened. She was gradually becoming more withdrawn too – she had severe learning difficulties, which made friendships difficult.

Joan had noticed how far away Christine seemed now. Normally she would be interested in what her mum was doing, watching her as she went about her usual morning chores, engaging with her, silently communicating with her in the way they did, that no one else could properly understand. But not any more. Now she looked away. She gazed out of the window. There was a stillness about her, a sadness, that unsettled Joan.

When Christine and David were settled, Joan fetched her phone book from the drawer and dialled a number. An appointment was made for the Saturday – still three days off. It almost felt too long to wait. Now she'd made up her mind to try something, she wanted it to happen immediately. 'I know it'll work,' she said to herself firmly, 'I know it will. It *has* to work.'

Joan's idea was to find Christine a companion cat. It was something she'd seen work with her own mum, when she'd been battling illness over many years. The old lady's cat had brought so much sunshine into her life, even in her bleakest moments. Joan hoped it might work for Christine too. But in order for that to happen, she would have to find a very special cat.

'This is the little tabby I had in mind, Mrs Payne.'

Joan had left Christine and her brother in the car with their dad, while she went in to meet the staff at the Cats Protection Adoption Centre. She'd visited a few times before. She loved cats. She loved their intelligence, their ability to sense feelings. Their independence. She knew how clever cats could be – and how comforting. Now she needed to find one that was all those things, and more. She needed a cat who would instinctively know how to stop a young girl from drifting into the darkness. A cat that would bring her back, and give her something to care about, to love, and be loved by. It was a lot to ask.

She looked at the cats in the pens, each with its own story – its own troubles, each desperate to find a home of its own.

'This is Speedy,' said the Cats Protection lady, pointing to a glass pen on the right-hand side.

At first glance, the name seemed wrong somehow. The small tabby cat in the pen didn't look like a rocket-fired feline! She was tiny and ladylike, a pretty little posh-paws.

'We don't know much about her,' said the lady sadly. 'She was found, like a lot of the others, straying from garden to garden. But I think she must have had a home at some stage, because when she gets to know you a bit, she can be quite loving.'

Joan looked at the little tabby, and wondered. Was this the cat she was looking for? Could it . . . would it change Christine's life? Then suddenly the cat turned and looked directly back at Joan, challenging her, almost, and she felt something stir inside her. Joan knew then. This *was* the one . . .

It wasn't quite so obvious to anyone else though, least of all Christine. For the first few days, Speedy did not take to anyone – certainly not Christine. She hid under beds. She lurked in corners. She came out to eat, or use her litter tray, then slunk back to the shadows, avoiding everyone.

Joan hoped she hadn't got it wrong. She'd already rehomed three other cats, each one a bois-terous, independent character – outdoorsy cats, who came in to eat, drink and rest a little, before heading off to hunt and play elsewhere. They weren't really interested in anyone, unless they were attached to a tin opener, and dishing up dinner!

Christine had noticed Speedy's arrival, of course. She took a great deal of interest in animals. They were her favourite things. She loved hearing animal stories – especially her dad's stories. He worked on a farm, where there were heavy horses, and she loved to hear about them. She liked looking at animals in picture books too, and on television; her eyes would light up when she saw a horse, or a dog, or a cat.

But Speedy wasn't particularly interested in her.

'What if I've made a mistake?' said Joan, as she sat with David on that first night. They watched the little cat as she darted out from under a cupboard and dashed into the kitchen to eat.

Speedy

'Well, her name suits her, anyway,' chuckled David. Then he saw how worried Joan looked, and his voice became more serious. 'Don't fret,' he said. 'It's bound to take her a few days to settle in. It's a strange house; lots of different smells and sounds. She'll soon get used to it, and get to know Christine.'

But what if she didn't? There was no way Joan could force the cat to care about Christine. Cats often favour the person who feeds them, but Christine wasn't able to do that. Nor could she offer Speedy cat treats. Or even cuddles. Her disability was such that she wasn't able to stroke or fuss over the cat, even if Speedy had wanted to be petted. 'She's *got* to be Christine's cat,' said Joan to herself. But how could she make it happen?

A week later everything changed.

It was late evening. Rain was pelting down outside, hammering against the windows. Joan was looking at a magazine, David was watching television, and Christine and her brother were both in their bedrooms. Suddenly Speedy shot into the living room, and started darting up and down the room, yowling loudly. Back and forward, up and down, agitated, disturbed.

Joan was shocked. It was the first time they'd heard the little cat make any sort of noise at all. And now this . . . as though the house was burning down!

'What's the matter, Speedy?' Joan tried to calm the cat, attempting to pick her up, but Speedy pulled away and carried on darting around the room, yowling and meowing, up and down, back and forward. Something had disturbed her greatly. But what?

Joan suddenly felt cold. 'I'm going to check on the kids,' she said to her husband.

By the time Joan reached her bedroom, Christine was lying on the floor.

Speedy

'David!' shouted Joan. 'Help me! Christine's having a seizure.'

Speedy got there before David. The small cat stood close to Christine, watching, waiting for the fit to stop. It seemed that now she had got Christine the attention she knew she needed, she would wait until whatever ailed her had passed.

Joan and David carefully cleared a space around Christine, so she couldn't hurt herself, and then did what they always did; talked softly and soothingly to her until it was all over.

Joan felt a lump in her throat as she glanced down at the little cat, resting now on her dainty paws, sitting as close to Christine as she could. Strangely, for the first time since she had arrived, Speedy didn't seem frightened. If anything, she had a protective look about her.

A little later, when Christine had recovered, and her parents had settled her safely in bed, Speedy jumped up beside her, snuggling softly into the warmth of Christine's side. Joan turned out the light, and lingered just a moment in the doorway, to watch them together. She saw how relaxed and peaceful Christine looked now, with Speedy close by. How had it happened? Why had Speedy chosen Christine, at that particular moment, just when she needed her most? People never chose cats, Joan knew that from experience. Cats always chose people. Had Speedy somehow sensed Christine's need, and been drawn to her? She certainly seemed to have realized Christine was in danger.

Over the next few months it happened again. And again. Each time Christine started to fit, Speedy would fetch Joan or David, and then stay close by Christine's side, until the fit had passed. As time went on, the little tabby even began to sense when a seizure was imminent and alert Joan, repeating the same pattern of pacing, darting and yowling to attract her attention – giving her just enough time to fetch Christine's medication, which helped ease the severity of the seizure a little. Joan was astonished. She couldn't believe what was happening. She almost held her breath when she watched them together, just in case the magic somehow disappeared . . .

And magic it certainly was. Christine was changing. She'd lost her faraway look, and in its place was a bloom, a freshness, a glow. Her face lit up when she saw Speedy, and the little cat, in turn, never strayed from her side. It was as though Speedy had finally found a home of her own and didn't want to leave it, even for a moment, in case it was taken from her and lost forever.

'They are like two lost souls who have found one another,' Joan thought to herself as she watched them one morning. Speedy was sitting in her now familiar place, on the top of Christine's high-backed chair. The little cat would have preferred her lap, but Christine's disability meant she was unable to hold her there – and after rolling off several times, Speedy had found a perch on the top of the chair instead, as close as she could to Christine's head.

Speedy was devoted to Christine, but she was still wary of other people. When the doctor called, Speedy kept her distance. She didn't like strangers in the house, and hated them being in Christine's room. She was happiest when they left. It was as though she feared they might take her away.

Winter finally gave way to spring, and Joan noticed the garden was starting to wake up from its slumber. That was another change, brought about by Speedy's arrival: Joan actually had a small amount of time to notice such things again. In the past Christine would have been anxious if her mum was out of sight – even just for a few moments – perhaps to hang washing on the line, or put rubbish in the bin. Now Joan could linger briefly to finish a job, without fear that Christine might be alarmed by her absence. Speedy had filled that gap too.

One bright sunny morning Joan was in the garden with Christine. Both were enjoying the warmth of the sun. Speedy was there too, of course, prancing around, chasing after a bee she'd spotted buzzing around the flowers. Christine liked watching the little cat's antics in the garden, but Speedy seldom strayed far from Christine's wheelchair. And Joan was glad. On the other side of the house was a busy road, and Speedy was far too precious to lose now.

Joan glanced down at the post that had arrived that morning, still unopened on her lap. It didn't look promising; a bank letter, a bill, a few supermarket flyers with their latest offers . . . and then something else altogether. A letter with a small cat logo on the front. Joan felt a flutter of excitement. Months back she'd entered a competition to find the country's most loyal cat. She'd written to the judges about Speedy, and how special she was to Christine. It was so long ago, Joan had forgotten all about it . . . With a shaking hand, she opened the letter, and read it through. And read it again, and a third time, just to be sure.

'Christine,' she said, with a gasp. 'You've won! You and Speedy have won an award – you've done it together!'

Christine could sense her mum's excitement, and her eyes shone with happiness – but in truth, she was far more interested in Speedy's antics. She turned her attention back to her cat, who was now leaping around the flowers, still trying to catch the bee.

Joan smiled as she watched her; Christine, her darling daughter, her brave child who had gone through so much, endured so much, and still had so many more difficult times ahead, was happy and content now, with her very own, special best friend. It was an award well won.

Noah

Kirsty glanced at her watch. The bus was already twenty minutes late. Another ten and they could safely assume it wasn't coming at all, and then: freedom! No school today.

It wasn't really a shock. Rain had fallen solidly for the last twenty-four hours, flooding streets and saturating the surrounding fields. Many roads were closed, bridges impassable, as swollen rivers burst their banks, and the drains choked back water. It was weird – coming as it had at the tail end of June.

All the kids in the village had been watching the television news closely, hoping it might mean a day off school. And now it looked like it might actually happen.

But just then a doleful shout came from somewhere further down the bus queue. 'There it is!' And then a communal groan, as ten necks craned to see the dark smudge of the high school bus appearing at the edge of the village.

But the game wasn't over yet. The bus was struggling, barely managing to force its way down the street through several feet of mud, sticks and rainwater. It reached them, but only just. As it opened its doors to let them on, a huge wave of water flushed up from the road, pouring in through the front of the bus, flooding the passageway and the driver's cab. It was the final straw for the driver. He held up his hand. 'Everyone off!' he said with a grimace. 'No bus today.' And no bus meant no school.

The kids were ecstatic. Kirsty and her pals were gripped with a sudden mad, holiday giddiness. For most of the year, the kids of the village moaned about how little there was to do. But not today! Living in the countryside suddenly had its benefits.

'Mum!' yelled Kirsty as she burst into the house. 'School's off! The bus can't get through!'

Her mum Julia wasn't really surprised. She'd been watching the news again, and the pictures of the floods were terrible.

'James will be *so* gutted,' giggled Kirsty as she flung her bag down and kicked off her shoes.

Her mum tried to frown – but it was true, he would be! James was Kirsty's younger brother, and still at primary school, just a short walk from their house. He was just as excited about the flooding as the rest of the village kids, and hadn't wanted to go to school. But unfortunately for him, he didn't need a bus to get to *his* school.

As she listened to Kirsty's tales of the flooded bus, and the swell of the water running through the village, Julia found herself getting caught up in the excitement.

'Come on,' she said a little later. 'Get your boots on, and we'll go take a look.'

Kirsty didn't need asking twice. In ten minutes they were on their way, out of the quiet cul-de-sac where they lived, and down towards the centre of the village.

They were only a few minutes from home when they noticed a commotion in one of the larger fields surrounding the village. A few horses had climbed on to a small bank of higher ground and were anxiously pacing, trying to keep out of the water. But it wasn't the horses that caught Kirsty's eye.

'I know those lads,' she said, pointing to a group of kids, wading through the waist-high waters that had flooded the field. She shivered – the water looked cold.

'What's going on?' her mum asked a lady

who was standing watching at the edge of the field.

'They've spotted some kittens,' she said. 'They're trying to get them out before they drown.'

'They've rescued one already,' said another lady.

Kirsty and her mum watched as the boys waded still deeper into the dark swelling waters.

'They're very brave,' said Julia softly.

Just then there was a shout from one of the boys. 'I've got another one!' And he held aloft a small black bundle. Then he began wading back to the edge of the field. Kirsty gasped as the lad stumbled slightly where the ground suddenly dipped, and the water became deeper. But he steadied himself and eventually trudged back to the shallower edges of the field. The little kitten in his hands mewed piteously.

'I'll take this one up to my granny's house,'

he said, holding the small body close to his dripping shirt.

Before anyone could stop him, he was off. Julia wondered if she should go after him, and make sure the kitten was all right. But just then they heard another shout. The man who owned the horses had arrived, and he was calling to the boys to come out of the water. But they were too busy to pay much attention. They'd found some bits of old timber, the remains of a chicken shed that had washed away in the water. Somehow they managed to lash together some of the pieces to form a makeshift raft. A few of them clambered aboard, slipping and falling, and then climbing back on again.

They pushed themselves out to the deepest part of the field. Kirsty held her breath, as they moved slowly around a patch of the ground, where a few tree branches jutted out of the water. Back and forward they went, the boys slipping off, then clambering back on again.

Bumble the Brave Kitten

'Be careful!' Kirsty's mum shouted. She really wanted them to come back now – it just wasn't safe – but then suddenly, a hand shot up . . .

'I've got it!'

Kirsty grabbed her mum's arm. 'Look!' she gasped.

The boy held a tiny bundle in his hand, even smaller than the last. Slowly, painfully slowly, the lads managed to push the raft back to the shallower parts of the field, one still clutching the kitten safely to his chest. They slid off the raft, then splashed through the shadows until they reached the watching crowd.

Julia found herself stepping forward to help the lad with the kitten as he came wearily over. 'I saw it clinging to a small branch,' he panted. 'It went under a few times, before I could grab it . . .'

'I'll take it,' said Julia gently, helping the lad out of the water. Relieved, he gladly handed the soggy bundle over.

58

Noah

At first she wasn't sure whether it was dead or alive. It was tiny, just bigger than her hand. Its black and white fur was sodden, its eyes closed, its skinny body freezing to the touch. She couldn't feel a heartbeat.

'I'll go home and fetch some towels,' said Kirsty, her voice trembling slightly. She could see how cold the kitten was.

As she dashed off, she heard one of the ladies who had been watching offer to fetch a washing basket to put the kitten in. Everyone was trying to help. Kirsty felt a knot of excitement growing in her stomach. Maybe they could keep the kitten . . . She'd always wanted a pet – a real pet. They'd had goldfish before, but nothing you could really cuddle – nothing that could actually share your world.

When she got back with the towels, her mum was holding the little scrap close to her, trying to transfer some of her own warmth into its tiny body. After a while, it opened its eyes, but still made no sound.

'It must be scared stiff,' she said, seeing Kirsty's worried face. 'It's a feral kitten – one of the ladies was telling me that she and her son were feeding them. That's how the boys knew they'd be here.'

Just then a couple of the lads reappeared, their clothes stuck to them, soaking and cold, but still full of energy. 'We haven't found the mum yet,' said one. 'Hopefully she's already escaped.'

Julia looked at the boy, his young face full of concern for the animals, and she felt very proud of him. Proud of all the lads. Teenagers, especially teenage boys, got such bad press . . . now she wished everyone in the village could see how brave these kids were. Heroes. Real heroes!

By the time they got the kitten home, Kirsty was already hopelessly attached to him. He was alert now, and his coat had dried out. He'd turned from a skinny bag-of-bones into a small fluffball with huge eyes. He was still traumatised, and very anxious, but there was something so appealing about him . . .

'Can we keep him, Mum?' said Kirsty softly. 'Please, Mum, we *have* to keep him.'

'We don't even know if he'll survive,' said Julia, trying not to get Kirsty's hopes up. 'And what will your dad say?' Scott, her husband, didn't like cats. He was allergic to them.

By the time Kirsty's brother James got home, the kitten was resting quietly in a cardboard box. As James stroked his soft fur, he felt the same instant bond as his sister.

'You can't just turn him out!' he said, appalled at the thought. 'Look at him, Mum!'

Julia looked. She looked at his tiny black body, his little white face, his pink nose. His big eyes and spiky fluffball coat.

Bumble the Brave Kitten

'We'll keep him tonight,' she sighed. 'And see what Dad says tomorrow.'

What would he say? Thankfully he was away on business that night, but tomorrow the kids would have to the face up to the fact that the kitten might not be allowed to stay.

Much later, as Kirsty turned out her light, she could hear the kitten crying pitifully downstairs. They'd put him in a snug little box in the utility room, but he was still very anxious. He wasn't used to people or the indoors; both scared him.

Kirsty shut her eyes tight. She had to resist the urge to creep down and comfort the little kitten – he was so wary of people, and petting and fussing made him worse. Instead, she turned her face into the pillow, and hoped the kitten would fall asleep soon. Tomorrow everything would work out, she knew it would.

★

Noah

By the next day the kitten was calmer, but still hadn't eaten anything. While Kirsty and James trudged miserably off to school, neither of them wanting to leave the kitten, Julia took him to the vet. Remarkably, after his brush with death, he got a clean bill of health. The vet said he was about six weeks old, had been weaned off his mum's milk and should be able to eat solid food. Julia was relieved. One of the ladies from the field had dropped off a few pouches of food from her own cats the night before, but despite her best efforts, the kitten wouldn't touch it. He was probably too shocked and exhausted to eat.

Thankfully the kitten wasn't suffering from cat flu, which according to the vet was rife among feral cats. The kitten also had a name. Noah. Kirsty and James had thought it up. And, given his adventures, it suited him well.

By teatime the kids were home, and they'd managed to coax the kitten into eating a little.

Bumble the Brave Kitten

Then they heard the key in the lock . . . Dad was back.

Julia had warned him, of course. She'd called him and told him they had an unexpected guest. He wasn't too pleased, but he was an animal lover and a great big softie at heart, so he wasn't really cross that they'd taken the little kitten in.

'So this is Noah, is it?' he said gruffly. Unlike the rest of the family, he didn't make a fuss of the kitten. After a quick glance, he ignored him, which was just the invitation Noah needed. He seemed strangely drawn to the children's father. He seemed to like his stillness, his peacefulness. When they sat down to eat, the kitten went to sit next to him.

Scott glanced at Noah when he thought no one else was looking. He was an attractive little scrap, and he felt his heart soften. Julia noticed, and tried not to smile.

Noah

'Can he stay, Dad?' said James, almost too nervous to ask.

'Please, Dad,' added Kirsty, a pleading look in her eye. 'It was meant to be – if Mum and I hadn't been passing, we'd never have seen him.'

'We'll see,' said their Dad gruffly, and the children knew then . . . they knew Noah would stay, forever.

The days and weeks passed, and Noah grew bigger, and stronger. And he lost his anxious eyes. He wasn't exactly a lap-cat – his first few weeks spent living as a feral cat had given him an instinctive wariness of people. But he loved his new family, just the same. And he soon fitted in. At first, Julia had tried to keep him out of the living room – she knew how much cats loved to scratch the furniture. But Noah didn't like to be apart from them. While they watched television together, he would cry outside the door. Julia instantly weakened, and Noah was allowed in. He immediately found a perch for himself, on top of a bookshelf. As time passed, he got used to being petted a bit, and he even enjoyed being stroked. His devotion to Scott continued. And it was mutual. A few months on, Noah got stuck inside a neighbour's garage. After a frantic search and a terrible night of worry, he was found, but it had been Scott who had worried the most. Soon after, he got a slight tummy bug . . . and again, it was Scott who fretted the most.

'I still don't like cats,' he told Julia and the kids when they teased him about it, 'but Noah's different!'

He certainly was different. And no one would ever forget where he'd come from, or how brave he'd been. Or, indeed, the bravery of the young lads who had saved his life. Julia contacted the local newspaper, and it printed a picture of the boys, holding Noah and his brothers. She was glad to see the boys finally getting the praise and attention they deserved.

That was the thing about Noah. Somehow he seemed to bring out the best in people. Julia and Kirsty often thought of that rainy, flooded June, when the young lads had shown their mettle, and how the local people had come together, pitched in to care for the kittens and help them. It showed what Julia had always known, that in times of crisis people pull together. It had just taken a lot of rain and some very soggy moggies to make it happen.

As the months passed, none of the family could remember life without Noah. Just as Kirsty had imagined, Noah shared their life fully. He would snooze on her bed, or sit with James, watching him while he played computer games. On sunny days he'd curl up in the garden or the conservatory – feeling the warmth through the glass on his beautiful sleek black coat.

Bumble the Brave Kitten

Strangely, after all he'd been through, he wasn't afraid of water. Like most cats, he didn't like being stuck in the rain — he much preferred staying indoors on damp days. But he loved to play with the stuff. The family would often see him sitting on top of the stone birdbath, pawing at the water, making little splashes and puddles. He did the same thing with his water dish inside. For a cat who had lost at least one of his nine lives because of water, it was odd behaviour. But then, perhaps he was just living up to his name.

Munchie

The old burned-out car had been abandoned months ago, left in a potholed siding off a busy dual carriageway. It was a wreck now, its windows smashed, the tyres gone. But there was still evidence of its old life; a few sweet wrappers in the footwell, a broken blue crayon on the back seat, and a child's comic charred from the fire, started by those who'd stolen it, half a year ago.

It was March now, and a small tabby cat, a feral female, heavy with kittens, had found the car. She'd crawled underneath into a small space, shelf-like, dry and hidden, close to the engine; a perfect place to make a nest for her kittens.

Barely a kitten herself, several of her young

didn't make it. They were too small, too weak, too cold. But the biggest kitten clung stubbornly to life. And the mother cat, for all her inexperience, was doing a good job of caring for him. He was putting on weight, and she was keeping close, making sure he was warm. Born blind and deaf as all kittens are, he was just nine days old when the men in the lorry arrived. The kitten's eyes were just starting to open, but hidden inside the car as he was, he couldn't see the men, nor could he hear them properly – his ears weren't fully developed yet. But his mother could . . .

The sudden roar of the lorry's engines, the squeal of its brakes and the shouting of the driver and his mate startled the young cat. And suddenly she was gone. Her kitten abandoned. Soon, he would have little memory of her; her warmth, her scent, the comfort and safety of being close to her. Now there was nothing but cold and noise.

'Lift the hoist up slowly,' said one man, tying chains around the body of the battered old car. 'That's it ... steady, there ... watch out; that exhaust's a goner ... a bit further ...'

The kitten could sense his mother had gone, but he was too young to follow her. He was help-less, still trapped in the car, as the men loaded it roughly on to the back of their huge lorry, where it joined several others, all of them old battered heaps, headed for the scrapyard. As they started up the engine, the kitten cried for his mother. But his lungs were small and his cries went unheard. Within minutes, the kitten and the car were gone.

Night fell. The car had been dumped in a pile at the scrapyard among the twisted heaps of metal and rubber. It would be crushed at first light.

Cold and hungry, the kitten instinctively still cried out for his mother, but every gasp made his thirst greater, and as the night's chill set in, his cries grew weaker. His mother wouldn't come, but others did. Several foxes, skinny and lithe, tripped lightly through the moonlit scrapyard, looking for rats. And more dangerous still, a mink with young of its own to feed slunk under the fence from the river beyond. Black and sleek, much bigger than a stoat, with sharp eyes and teeth, it prowled round the outer fence, searching for prey . . . and then suddenly it stopped. It had heard the kitten's cries.

Alert now to the scent of the small cat, the mink circled the car. A young kitten would make a good meal for the mink and its family. The kitten was silent now, almost as though he sensed the danger. But the mink could still smell him. It stole under the car, just a breath away from the kitten . . . and then a vole suddenly shot across the mink's path, distracting it. The vole stopped dead in its tracks, frozen with fear. It realized the

danger too late. The mink made a lunge for it –
and the kitten was spared.

Hours later, dawn came at last. And the kitten
still clung weakly to life. He wasn't able to cry
much now. Severely dehydrated, he would die
soon, perhaps even before the crusher got to the
car.

Bill had worked at the scrapyard for ten years. He
operated the crane that manoeuvred the cars into
the crusher, where they were reduced to flattened
metal envelopes. From his cab – some fifteen feet
off the ground – he had a good view of the yard.
And he enjoyed watching the wildlife that thrived
among the scrap.

He was also a bit of a car nut. He liked to
tinker, and get his hands dirty – rebuilding old
bangers from scrap he'd found at the yard. Most
of the spare parts he used to patch them up had
been salvaged there. That was the joy of the

place: you never knew what you might find.

It was a cold morning. Bill gulped down his mug of tea, thick with milk and sugar. It burned his throat a bit, but the warmth spreading through him felt good. He took a final slug, then put on his hat and clumped heavily out of the portacabin to start work.

Inside the old red car, the kitten was too weak to move. His eyes closed, his mouth dry, every swallow a razor blade on his parched throat. He vaguely heard the sound of Bill's crane starting up, and the shuddering clunk, as it attached itself to the car. But he was losing consciousness rapidly, his senses shutting down. And then suddenly, there was a jolt. The crane had taken the strain of the car and begun lifting it. The kitten was shunted roughly to one side as the car rose upward, spinning slightly. The sudden movement woke the kitten, and instinctively, with the last breath he had in his tiny body, he cried out again for his mother.

Pitifully quiet, he mewed, once, twice . . . a third time maybe, while the car continued to rise, creaking and shuddering, skywards.

The sun was shining, the birds were singing, and Bill congratulated himself for the millionth time for having a job he enjoyed. He couldn't understand anyone choosing to work in an office. He glanced down and noticed a pair of cheeky wagtails, prancing around on the ground below him, and he grinned. And then suddenly he heard it: a faint high-pitched cry. At first he thought he'd imagined it, and carried on with the job, swinging the red car dangerously close to the enormous jaws of the crusher. Then he heard it again.

Bill stopped. He put the hoist brakes on, and turned off the engine, and listened harder. It was clearer now. He started to get a slightly sick feeling in his belly. He'd heard that sound before. He tried to place it . . . then he remembered. A year

Bumble the Brave Kitten

or so back, his sister's cat had had kittens. He remembered the high-pitched cries of the newborns, not unlike a human baby. And there was something else too. He remembered his sister's cat had chosen to give birth somewhere dark, and secret, where no one would find her babies. He looked at the red car again, still swaying in the breeze. Then he fumbled for the starter, and the engine roared back into life. But this time, he lowered the car down. He jumped out of the cab. The cries had stopped now, but there was another sound – much softer – a rasping breath, barely audible over the distant thrum of a lorry, working on the other side of the yard. Bill hastily untied the chains on the car, and threw open the bonnet. And he found the kitten. Small. Desperately small, covered in engine oil, his eyes blinking at the brightness of the light suddenly upon him.

Bill stood and gaped, and for a second or two

he wasn't sure what to do. Then he bent down, scooped up the tiny cat in one enormous hand, and carried him back to the office.

'His eyes are open, so he's probably about ten days old,' said the gentle veterinary nurse, holding the little kitten in her soft hand. 'How he survived for so long without his mum is beyond me.'

It wasn't Bill who had taken him to the vet's; it was the foreman of the yard, Albert. When Bill had appeared in the office, his face ashen, the tiny kitten still held close to his chest, Albert had melted. He was a big-hearted old man with a huge bushy beard. An animal lover himself, he already had a couple of cats and dogs at home. He looked at the kitten and realized the little fella was close to death. If he was to stand a chance of surviving, he needed help straight away. Albert put him in a cardboard box, and drove him to the vet's himself. Even before he got there, he'd made up his mind: if the kitten made it, he'd give him a home.

Veterinary nurse Kersty Ellis had been changing dressings in the recovery room when Albert arrived, the kitten hunched in the corner of the box he carried. An experienced nurse, she'd hand-reared many newborn kittens before, but she'd never seen one this sickly survive. She wasn't giving up on him.

She fetched a small bottle, and some kitten milk, and put a few drops in his mouth. Weak as he was, his sucking reflex was still there, and he managed to swallow a few sips.

'That's a good sign,' she told Albert, still waiting by her side. 'He's a fighter!'

Just then the kitten started to mew loudly for more milk.

'And he's got a good pair of lungs too!' she added with a smile.

Albert glanced at the clock. He had to get back

to the yard, but he promised to return the following day. He gave the kitten a little tickle under the chin before leaving.

After the kitten had had a thorough check-up from the vet, Kersty fetched the soap and water. The tiny cat's coat was black and stiff with engine oil. It was on his eyes and his mouth too. Kersty gently sponged it off, while the kitten protested loudly. He'd certainly found his voice, which Kersty knew was a good sign. It took quite a bit of cleaning, but gradually his true colour began to show through. He was a beautiful little tabby and white.

A few hours later the kitten was wrapped in a towel, his coat fluffed up and his belly full of milk. Kersty put him in one of the surgery pens, and watched him nod off to sleep, snoring softly. The little bundle had touched her deeply. She sighed. That was the problem with working in the vet's — it was hard to resist any animal in need. She stroked

the tiny kitten's head, and talked softly to him.
'Don't worry, little man, I'll look after you.'

But hand-rearing a newborn kitten is no easy
task, especially one so weak. For the first few
weeks he would need constant feeding – every
two hours or so, day *and* night! But Kersty was
prepared to try. She took the kitten home with
her when the surgery closed, and at bedtime she
set her alarm clock, ready for the first feed. Not
that she needed it. The kitten woke her up himself
every couple of hours, mewing loudly when he
was hungry. And he was hungry a lot. He seemed
to be making up for the lack of food he'd had in
the last few days.

'You're a right little muncher,' Kersty mumbled
as she gave him his 2 a.m. bottle. Then she giggled.
Munchie! That was what she should call him. The
name suited him well.

A few hours later, as Kersty got up for work,
bleary-eyed and exhausted, she realized how

attached she'd become to the little kitten. And the kitten, in turn, had found a new mum. They became inseparable. The kitten went to work with Kersty each day, so she could feed him regularly. He liked being at the vet's. He liked the noise, and the attention. Munchie spent so much time at the vet's that he became comfortable around all types of animals, from rabbits and guinea pigs to other cats and dogs. And he got used to people too; children and adults. Nothing fazed him.

Meanwhile, Albert kept his word. He visited Munchie every day, giving him loads of cuddles and attention.

It was a sunny afternoon several weeks later. Munchie was stronger now. Kersty had been able to cut back his night-time feeds, and he was thriving. His coat was shiny. His eyes were bright. The sickly little kitten discovered in the scrapyard had become a cuddly and playful little fluffball.

Albert was visiting, as usual. He was tickling Munchie behind the ears and chatting away to him, while Kersty went about her work behind him.

'A few more weeks here, lad,' said Albert, lovingly stroking the kitten, 'and then I'll take you home with me.'

Kersty froze. She'd known Albert loved the kitten, and had planned to take him home when he was strong enough – but now the time was close, she suddenly couldn't bear to part with him. Albert saw the look on her face, and understood instantly. He saw how attached the nurse had grown to the kitten. He smiled at her.

'It's OK,' he said simply. 'Munchie can stay with you.'

Relief flooded through Kersty. He was one of her family now.

Munchie

As the weeks passed, Munchie continued to grow bigger and stronger. And eventually he was old enough to stay at home while Kersty was at work. He didn't mind too much. He'd been accepted quickly by Kersty's other pets – Molly, another rescue cat, was a particular chum, and the pair regularly curled up together.

A year later and Munchie was fully grown. He'd turned into a big and very loving cat. He liked to be petted and cuddled, and he was living up to his name. He was never happier than when he was eating. He'd even pinch the other cats' food, given half a chance! It was almost as if he felt he had to stock up on food, just in case he fell on lean times again.

Kersty smiled when she remembered how she'd first seen him – a skinny little scrap from the scrapyard! Weak and sickly and close to death. Now he was a strapping tom cat, with a big heart and an appetite to match. But as much as she loved him, and his big chunky tummy, it was time for some tough love. In future, there would be fewer munchies for Munchie. The skinny little scrap-yard cat, who'd turned into a mighty-tummed tom, was now officially on a diet!

Mr Ginge

The little cat was desperate now. Her time was close. And yet still she waited, watching carefully as the large metal doors to the elephant house slowly swung open. It was a sunny morning at Colchester Zoo. The cat could feel the replenishing warmth of the sun's rays spreading through her fur, chasing away the night chills. But she didn't have time to enjoy it. She was urgently seeking the darkness now; a shady refuge where she could give birth to her kittens.

She watched as the first elephants emerged. A female named Tanya, the dominant cow of the herd, followed quickly by her five-year-old calf. Then two more females and a younger calf.

Tembo, the largest elephant, wasn't there. He had his own area now, and just as he would have done in the wild, he spent most of his time away from the herd.

The cat watched unafraid as the mighty giants edged out into the paddock, each claiming their favourite places, and the calves cavorted playfully around their huge feet. She had a healthy respect for the animals – keeping her distance and respecting their space – but she wasn't scared of them. She was familiar with their smells and sounds. And the riches from living among them were plenty: lots of rats and mice who were attracted by the animals' food.

But she wasn't interested in hunting now. She was waiting. She had to be sure the elephants were occupied, and the keepers even more so. She had to be certain no one would see her before she could go to her secret place. She'd found it days ago – a workroom hidden beneath the elephant house where the keepers kept their tools. It was dry and dark, and safe – perfect for her needs. But getting in was a problem. To reach it, she had to go through the middle of the large outdoor paddock, almost under the noses of the elephants, then pass through the huge doors into the elephant house itself where the keepers were already hard at work on their morning chores. And then finally, if she got that far, she could slink down a stairwell to the workroom.

Within the hour, she got her chance. One of the female elephants, Zola – the most high-spirited of the adults – had suddenly broken into a skittish trot around the paddock, raising her trunk high and kicking up the dust with her huge feet. A few early visitors watched her antics delightedly. And while all eyes were on Zola, the little cat passed through unnoticed.

She made for the big doors: a swift streak of fur, creeping low in the shadows. The elephant

Bumble the Brave Kitten

smell inside was almost a comfort to her. She noticed one of the keepers working there, head down, engrossed in his work. The cat crept silently past him, to the doorway leading down to the workroom. She was close now . . . but then she almost failed at the final hurdle. A keeper suddenly emerged from another room, carrying a huge bucket of fruit. The cat froze into the shadows, and the keeper didn't spot her.

She had made it. Hours later, as she lay waiting in the quiet darkness of the workroom, she heard the noises of the elephants above her, preparing to bed down for the night.

Mick Harrison had been an elephant keeper at the zoo for five years. He loved his job, especially the animals. The elephants never failed to delight and amaze; big and bulky, yet playful, gentle, often sensitive, always intelligent. Each had their own likes and dislikes, and odd little foibles. Just like people, really.

Mick was weary now though. It had been a long day. There had been several coach parties visiting the zoo – large groups of school kids full of chatter and questions. The keepers secretly loved it. They enjoyed sharing their knowledge, of course, but more than that, they liked to watch the effect the elephants had on people. They liked to see the wonder on their faces, especially the kids. There was something about the elephants that seemed to touch everyone who saw them. Of course, all the zoo keepers felt that way about their animals – but Mick *knew* it was true about the elephants. They were special.

Slowly Mick finished sweeping up the workroom. It wasn't a bad job – the peace and quiet of the room was quite relaxing after a busy day outside with the noise and hustle and bustle. He was lost in his own thoughts, gently moving aside the boxes and bins that stood at the far end of the room, as he gave it a thorough clean up.

Bumble the Brave Kitten

He was nearly finished, and there was just one more bin to move and clean behind. He put down his brush, and pulled back the bin, and then . . . froze. He caught his breath. There, in amongst the darkness and dust, barely noticeable in the shadows, curled up tightly together on an old sack, was a tiny bundle of bodies. Newborn kittens. There was a moment of utter stillness as Mick looked at them. He couldn't tear his eyes away – it was such a shock to find life in that dusty old room. For a moment he looked without really registering what he was seeing. Then a noise from above – another keeper moving sacks, perhaps – woke him from his momentary stupor. He looked more closely. There were five of them. All tiny dark shapes, except for the one in the middle, which was orange. He smiled when he saw the brightness of its marmalade-coloured coat. Mick was ginger-haired himself, and had a fondness for all things orange!

Tizer

Left: Tizer and Inspector Roy at King's Cross Police Station; *below:* Tizer enjoying his retirement

Stewie

Above, bottom left: fundraising for Stewie's treatment; *above, top right*: Stewie with Ruby and Jacob

Speedy

Far right: Speedy and Christine

Noah

Top left: moments after his rescue; *top right*: flooded Methley, 2007; *middle left*: Noah and James; *middle right*: Noah with one of his brave rescuers, Aiden Wright; *bottom left*: Noah and Kirsty

Munchie

Munchie and Kersty

Mr Ginge

Top right: Mr Ginge with Head Elephant Keeper Claire Bennett; *below right*: inside the Elephant House at Colchester Zoo, where Mr Ginge was born

Marmite

Marmite with baby Ruby

Felix

Right: Felix and Mandy

Donna

Donna – a home of her own at last

Bumble

Brave-heart Bumble

Mr Ginge

Mick didn't know much about cats, but he could tell these were very new. Their eyes were far from opening. They barely moved, though he could see them breathing when he looked closer. He had one last glance, smiling again at the little ginger kitten, and then quickly, instinctively, replaced the bin, and retreated. He didn't want to scare off the mother, who would no doubt return soon. If she found her nest disturbed, there was a danger she might abandon the kittens. Mick edged away, and quietly left the room. Strangely, he felt a slight knot of excitement in his stomach.

He went off to find the head keeper, who was working upstairs. 'There's a litter of kittens in the workroom,' he said. 'And I'd like to have the ginger one — I mean, eventually, when they're old enough to need a home . . .'

Claire Bennett, the head keeper, was shocked. And so was Mick! He had no idea what had made him say that. He didn't even like cats! He was a dog person, for goodness sake. And he certainly wasn't looking for a pet. And yet, there was something about that tiny little ginger scrap that had touched him deeply. He sensed they were meant to be together. He knew it in his bones!

Litters of feral kittens weren't unusual at the zoo, but this was the first time one had been found so close to the animals. Although the cats weren't encouraged, they were tolerated by the keepers, accepted even, because they were experts at pest control. They kept the rat population to a minimum. In return the keepers did their best to keep the cats healthy – and new kittens gave them a good opportunity to do just that. In the past they'd worked with Cats Protection, who would collect both the mother and her kittens and vaccinate and neuter them.

That was the plan this time too, and Mick was sorry he wouldn't be there to see it. He was going on leave for a couple of days, though he promised to call and remind them that he wanted to stake a claim for the ginger kitten! Claire smiled at that. She hadn't expected Mick to be such a big softie where kittens were concerned . . .

It was late morning the following day when Claire and another keeper, Angela, caught sight of the mother cat, padding quickly across the elephant house. The keepers knew it was important to catch the mother cat as well as her kittens. If she abandoned them now, it could be fatal for the litter. Claire checked her watch – it would be a while before the Cats Protection people arrived. By then it could be too late.

Angela offered to catch the mum-cat herself. She was an experienced keeper who had spent years working with wild animals. Catching a small cat shouldn't be too much of a problem.

As soon as Angela approached her, the cat was defensive and backed away, hissing and spitting.

Bumble the Brave Kitten

Feral cats are instinctively wary of humans, and this one was more anxious than normal, with her kittens close by. Angela moved towards her slowly, talking softly. The keeper was calm, and gentle. She was used to making animals feel at ease. But it did no good. As she bent down, the little cat turned on her, ears flat, claws out, hissing loudly, and bit and scratched the keeper badly.

Angela struggled with her, trying to free her stinging hand from the animal's sharp teeth. But the cat wouldn't release her. After a brief tussle, Angela managed to prise open the cat's jaws, and remove her hand. She backed off, while the cat continued arching her back and hissing threateningly.

Angela's hand was badly damaged, and her good intentions were in vain. Now they'd take their chances, and hope the people from Cats Protection would have better luck.

Thankfully, they did. Perhaps the cat had spent all her energy on the poor keeper who had been trying to help her. Whatever the reason, she put up little resistance when they trapped her, and they removed both the mother cat and the kittens later that day. Their zoo adventure had ended.

Mick, meanwhile, kept to his word. Claire was barely back in her office when the phone rang again. 'Did you tell them?' he said anxiously. 'Did you tell them I want the ginger one?'

Claire grinned. She *had* told them, and they were glad to hear it. Already having a home for one of the kittens was a boost. It was kitten season, and the Adoption Centres were full.

All the zoo kittens would eventually be rehomed, and even the mum-cat, whom they named Nellie, was eventually rehomed to a nearby farm – the perfect environment for a feral cat.

★

Bumble the Brave Kitten

Over the next few weeks Mick kept in close contact with the charity. And eventually the kitten was old enough for him to visit. He felt an instant bond with the little orange bundle. Unlike his mum, the kitten was already used to humans. The foster carers at Cats Protection had made sure he wasn't afraid of people, with lots of handling and human attention. The kitten was now a fluffy little ball of fun, and thoroughly enjoyed Mick's visits, playing with him, wrestling and chasing toys.

The weeks passed quickly, and soon it was time to take him home. Mick was delighted. He'd got everything ready for him – including a name. Mr Ginge!

The plan was for him to be an indoor cat. At the time Mick was living in a cottage next door to the zoo – perfect for work, but not so ideal for a cat. It was on a busy road, much too dangerous to let Mr Ginge out.

The kitten settled well at first, and quickly became close to Mick. But as the weeks went on, Mick became worried about him. When he was out at work the young cat would get up to all sorts of mischief: pulling off wallpaper, scratching the furniture, pulling up the carpet, ripping paper, trying to open cupboards. And he played rough too. The gentle little ball of fluff had turned into a teenage hoodlum, wrestling, biting and scratching. Mick was at a loss. He even wondered whether it was the kitten's feral roots starting to show. But then fate stepped in. Mick fell in love. And Sarah his partner didn't just fall for one ginger lad – she fell for the little orange cat too.

An experienced cat owner herself, Sarah had hand-reared two of her own, when their mum died soon after they were born. When Sarah and Mick eventually set up home together, in a house further away from the zoo, Mr Ginge changed almost overnight. Suddenly he had access to a big garden, with fields beyond, and an outdoor cat pen to shelter in when Sarah and Mick were at work. He also had a couple of playmates – Sarah's cats, Minxy and Shady, who took to Mr Ginge quickly. As a result, his behaviour changed for the better. And Mick realized it had been boredom and lack of a garden that had probably been the cause of Mr Ginge's bad habits. Now he was a model cat, though still a big and boisterous character, often landing himself in trouble with his curiosity and mischievous nature. He often dashed inside the cat food cupboard, when Sarah or Mick opened it to find a tin – and much later they'd hear tapping, or banging, and find Mr Ginge trapped inside!

But with his big personality came a big amount of love too. While Minxy and Shady were content to settle down at night at the bottom of the couple's bed, Mr Ginge wouldn't be happy until he was right under the covers next to them, occasionally taking a playful swipe at an unsuspecting toe or two. You could take the cat out of the zoo, but not the zoo out of the cat!

Marmite

Breathe! she told herself. *Come on, Lindsey, breathe through it.* She clutched the edge of the table, her knuckles white and straining, as another intense contraction rippled through her body. She tried to focus, just like they'd learned at class, but it was so difficult to concentrate on anything. And then she realized she was holding her breath again. *Breathe!* she almost yelled at herself. Then she felt a soft face nuzzling its way under her arm, and a big long tail batted her in the face. Lindsey grinned, the tension evaporating, and as the contraction passed, she laughed out loud.

'Hello, boy,' she said breathlessly. 'It's a good

job you're here, or I'd be worrying myself stupid!'

The cat responded affectionately, nuzzling into her side, trying to climb on her lap, though it was nearly impossible; Lindsey was just hours from having a baby, and her bump took up most of the space on the chair.

She glanced at the clock again. Where was Huw? Her husband had set out for the supermarket a few hours ago, to stock up before the baby came, and he still wasn't back. If he didn't hurry up, thought Lindsey, he'd miss the whole thing! She picked up her mobile again and tried his number, but the signal wasn't great at the best of times, and she still couldn't reach him. She threw it on the floor in frustration.

'It's just you and me then, Marmite,' she said, sighing. The cat meowed a reply, as though he understood every word. Secretly Lindsey thought he probably did. He was a very understanding cat, a real comfort to her. And if Huw didn't make it back for the birth, then as far as Lindsey was concerned, Marmite was the next best thing!

She buried her face in his fur and sniffed the delicious fresh air smell he always had. She loved that smell — it was as though he brought the garden in with him. It immediately relaxed her.

Lindsey had wanted a cat for a long time but, what with work and a busy life with lots of friends and family, she hadn't got round to finding one. And then, with just a few months to go before her baby arrived, she'd woken up one morning and announced the time had come to get a cat! Huw was a bit shocked. He thought there was plenty going on already. But he knew better than to argue with a pregnant lady! And besides, Lindsey had had a really tough time of it lately. Several serious health complaints had dogged her pregnancy, leaving her exhausted and very weak. And as it turned out, the cat couldn't have come at a better time. She was signed off from work, too poorly to carry on, and was suddenly faced with three months home alone – confined to the sofa until her baby came. Marmite was a godsend.

'What shall we do now?' said Lindsey, tickling the cat under his chin. 'The books all say I'm supposed to keep busy in between contractions – so shall we watch telly, or read a magazine . . .' Marmite looked back at her, almost with a shrug, and then cuddled in closer. 'Suits me,' said Lindsey, softly stroking his jet-black fur.

Marmite was a rescue cat – just six months old when they got him. The Adoption Centre wasn't sure where he'd come from; he was a stray when they found him. But Lindsey suspected that at some point he'd been badly treated. Sometimes when you raised your hand to turn off a light, or reach for something, he'd cower away as though he felt you were about to hit him. And he was a real homebody too – preferring to stay close to Lindsey, whom he adored from the start.

'Well, we're in a right pickle now, boy, aren't we?' said Lindsey, still stroking the now purring cat. 'So much for just a twinge . . .' She smiled despite herself.

That's how it had started. When she'd got up that morning, she'd mentioned to Huw that she had an ache in her back, and had felt a few twinges in her tummy. But it was their first baby, and neither of them knew whether this was the real thing. She was already six days over her due date, but the midwife had warned her it might still be another week or so before the baby decided to make an appearance. All the same, Huw was concerned. Just before he'd set out for the supermarket, he hesitated in the doorway, wondering whether he should go at all. 'What if the baby comes?' he'd said, white-faced and worried.

But Lindsey had just laughed. 'Don't be

daft – first babies always take hours to come! If this *is* labour, we'll probably still be waiting for the real action to start by bedtime – and anyway, we're almost out of milk and teabags!'

They'd both giggled then. And Huw had left with a light heart. But half an hour after he'd gone, suddenly everything had changed. Suddenly the twinges had become aches, and the aches had developed quickly into proper labour pains that were growing stronger and more frequent. And Lindsey knew instinctively that this was it – the baby was coming soon. She was excited and nail-bitingly nervous, all at the same time.

She suddenly stiffened, and then braced herself. 'Here we go again . . .' she said, feeling another contraction starting. She gripped the table again – it seemed to help to have something firm to grab on to – and closed her eyes. Marmite, still by her side, squashed even closer against her. He was quiet and calm, a solid rock for her to lean against. Lindsey could feel his warmth radiating through her. It made her feel calmer having him so close, and it was just as well. This contraction was even stronger than the last. She gritted her teeth. But it was OK, she would cope – she wasn't alone now, Marmite was with her. And he stayed there, solidly, steadfastly close to her, almost as though he was trying to absorb some of the tension from her. Eventually it passed. And almost immediately, Marmite started talking again. He did that a lot – he was a very chatty cat. He meowed to her questioningly, as though asking whether she was all right now.

'I'm fine,' panted Lindsey, gasping for breath. She took a few deep gulps of air, and began to feel normal again. Marmite, meanwhile, jumped down from the chair and walked around the room a few times, as though he was checking everything was in order.

'Good idea!' said Lindsey, hauling herself up

out of the chair to join him. 'The midwife told me to keep moving when it started.'

But she didn't move far — just to the kitchen to make a cup of tea. She was trying to remember what they'd told her in her antenatal classes — wasn't there something about having something to eat so you had loads of energy? But she couldn't face food. 'I'd best try to eat something,' she said as Marmite padded through to join her. She took a slice of bread and returned to her chair. But the thought of it turned her stomach. She abandoned the bread on the table. Marmite's eyes twinkled. He loved bread! He jumped up and sneaked a nibble. Lindsey tried to look cross, but it was impossible. And anyway, he'd only nip over the neighbour's fence and pinch the stuff she put out for the birds . . . he did that most mornings.

She glanced at the clock; another hour gone. Where was Huw? She was beginning to worry now. Soon, very soon, she would need to go to hospital. Marmite was great for moral support, but he couldn't exactly call an ambulance, or drive her there! And what if the baby came so quickly that it arrived before the ambulance? Marmite was watching her now, and as though sensing her concern, he piped up again, meowing loudly . . . Then he jumped up next to her, snuggling close.

'Yeah, I know,' said Lindsey, feeling immediately calmer again. 'You're here, and it'll all be all right.' Somehow it always was when Marmite was around. He seemed to know exactly how to make things better. Whenever Lindsey was worried, or ill, he would stay close, cuddling up, chatting to her and taking her mind off whatever was bothering her. And now he seemed to realize she needed him even more than usual.

Just then she felt it coming again. She checked her watch; the contractions were getting closer together now, and stronger. Her labour was moving fast. Very soon her life would change dramatically. Very soon, she'd be a mum.

'A boy or a girl?' she said through gritted teeth, as the contraction gripped her again. But Marmite didn't have the chance to answer, because just then they heard a key in the lock.

'Lindsey?'

Huw appeared in the doorway, weighed down with shopping. He took in the scene – his wife, as white as sheet, gripping the edge of the table, her teeth clenched, her eyes closed, and Marmite, looking serious and supportive by her side. The shopping bags were abandoned, milk, bread, apples spilling out on the floor as Huw rushed over to Lindsey's side – a huge wave of excitement and anxiety sweeping over him.

He realized immediately: it was time.

Hours later, Huw returned to the house and found Marmite waiting nervously in the hall. He was obviously on edge. When they'd left for the hospital Marmite had been reluctant to let Lindsey go. And she'd have gladly taken him with her.

'I don't see why I can't,' she'd grumbled. 'Other people get to take favourite things: cushions, blankets, CDs . . .'

Huw raised his eyebrows. 'They don't take their pets!'

'But Marmite's my comfort blanket – he relaxes me.'

Eventually Huw had prised them apart, and they'd left for hospital. And hours later, Lindsey had given birth to a girl: Ruby.

'Don't worry, boy, they're both fine,' said Huw, stroking the cat's soft head.

Marmite peered at him closely; he could sense Huw was happy. Reassured, he padded off to the kitchen for his dinner.

Later, as Huw crawled into bed, utterly exhausted, Marmite followed him. It was a habit he'd picked up when they'd first got him. He'd been much smaller then, just a big kitten, really, but even now, fully grown and a big lad, he still liked to snuggle up with them at night. It was always a bit of a squeeze, especially as Marmite wriggled so much. But not tonight. Lindsey and the baby would be in hospital for a few days. Until then the boys had the bed to themselves. Soon they were asleep; peaceful and snoring.

'But what if he doesn't like her . . .'

It was three days later, and Huw was bringing Lindsey and baby Ruby home from hospital.

'I mean, what if she scares him? She's quite loud when she cries . . .'

Huw grinned at his wife. It was typical of Lindsey to be worrying about everyone, including the cat!

Lindsey was sitting in the back seat next to Ruby. She couldn't stop looking at her baby. She was so perfect. Tiny fingers, long eyelashes, beautiful big eyes – and a pretty big pair of lungs too. When she was hungry, the whole world knew about it!

'Don't worry, Marmite will get used to her,' said Huw, turning into their street. Huw certainly had. Already both he and Lindsey couldn't remember life without their lovely little Ruby.

'It'll be so good to be home,' sighed Lindsey as they reached their house. She'd signed herself out of hospital a day early. It was just too loud and busy there, and she longed for the peace and calm of her own house, a place where she and Ruby could rest and get to know one another properly. And then, of course, there was Marmite. Lindsey had missed him loads. She couldn't wait to stroke his silky coat and see his happy face again. But in the back of her mind was a worry – what if he was jealous of Ruby? Or worse, what if he was mean to her? For so long now, it had just been the three of them, and now they were four . . .

As soon as they arrived, Marmite came running. He was ecstatic to see Lindsey. So much so that at first he barely noticed baby Ruby. But then Huw set the car seat down in the middle of the living room, and Marmite's nose got the better of him. He looked long and carefully. Then he walked all the way round the seat, twice. Then he gave it a sniff, sat back and looked up at Lindsey enquiringly.

'This is Ruby,' she said, smiling at him. Just then, the baby opened her eyes and let out a loud, ear-splitting cry as only newborns are capable of. Marmite nearly fell over with shock! He jumped to his feet, and ran and hid behind the sofa. It took a fair bit of coaxing to get him out again.

But Huw was right. Marmite adapted quickly. And as the days passed he became fond of the baby, almost protective of her – like a big brother. At any time of the day, or night, if Ruby woke up and started crying, Marmite would howl too, and go and fetch Lindsey – yowling until she followed him to the baby. And whenever people came to visit, Marmite liked to stay close to Ruby, fixing them with a serious stare, almost as though he was keeping her safe. Ruby, for her part, was fascinated by the cat. She watched him constantly. Her eyes followed him as he chased around the room, playing with toys, or rolling in the sunshine. Jealousy wasn't a problem at all – though Lindsey noticed that Marmite saved up all his best antics for the times Ruby was having a cuddle. It was a bit like having an older toddler in the house, who liked to make sure he was getting some attention too!

It was a sunny Saturday morning a few months after Ruby was born. Lindsey was sitting with the baby in the living room, and Huw was glancing through a newspaper, when suddenly they heard a tinkling noise. Then Marmite appeared, chasing a small red ball with a tiny bell inside. He batted it around the room for a bit, chasing it back and forward, up and down, before eventually picking it up in his mouth and dropping it on the sofa next to the baby.

'Awww, look, Huw,' said Lindsey. 'Marmite's brought Ruby his toy. Isn't that lovely . . .'

Huw glanced up from his paper and frowned. 'Yes, that's really thoughtful of him, but the only problem is, it isn't *his* toy . . .' He grinned. 'It belongs to one of the new kittens next door, and that's the third time he's pinched it this week!'

Felix

Summer was slipping softly into autumn. The ripe corn stood tall in the fields, waving gently in the breeze, as if beckoning the farmers to get on with the harvest. The mice had already started theirs, gorging themselves on the plump corn. And where there are mice, there are cats . . .

Felix and Jasper were brothers. Young and strong, with sleek black and white fur, they spent the summer days chasing mice in the fields behind their house. Felix was the faster of the two. When he caught the scent of a mouse, nothing would distract him.

As dusk fell one late September afternoon, he caught a strong scent. Head down, tail up, he chased the mouse, hither and thither through the sheaves of corn. The mouse was fast, but Felix was faster. And he nearly had it, but then it turned sharply in the opposite direction, momentarily throwing the cat off course.

Somewhere in the distance Felix was aware of the sound of heavy machinery. A combine harvester had begun work earlier that day, cutting and sorting the corn, but Felix was keeping a safe distance away.

Then the wind changed direction, and the heavy chugging of the machine was suddenly closer. Felix briefly lost sight of the mouse and hesitated, then spotted it again, and gave chase once more. He could hear the combine harvester more clearly now, though it still seemed far away.

The mouse darted off to the left, but Felix was on its tail. Faster, faster he streaked through the corn, chasing the rodent, just a breath away from catching it. Then he stopped. The thrashing noise of the machine was suddenly very close by. The mouse had gone. Felix tried to escape from the noise. But as the wind began to pick up he was having trouble working out exactly where the combine harvester was. He darted forwards, and then with a start, realized he'd turned straight into its path. The machine's whirring silver blades mesmerized him. He panicked. Too late, he tried to jump aside, but the combine harvester was much too wide, too quick for him. And for Felix, everything suddenly stopped.

The evening was warm enough to have the car windows down. Mandy and Frank Parsall were enjoying a leisurely drive home, after a family party. It had been a good day, but they were tired. Mandy's feet ached, and Frank was looking forward to the peace of their cosy living room, the Sunday papers, and a nice cup of tea in his favourite chair.

Felix

Carefully Frank reversed the car into their drive. Mandy immediately caught sight of Jasper – one of their cats. Both Jasper and Felix knew the sound of the Parsalls' car, and were usually waiting for them on the doorstep by the time they'd parked up and got out.

'I don't see Felix,' said Mandy, as Jasper fussed around her ankles.

Frank smiled. 'He's probably after a mouse somewhere. He's bound to hear the tin opener though. He'll be back before you've had time to put his tea out!'

Mandy grinned. Felix, like most cats, was ruled by his stomach. He never missed a meal.

But this time, he didn't appear.

Mandy and Frank both called for him. They called and called. They walked down to the fields, silent now, the farmer long since finished for the day. They called again. There was still no sign of Felix. Frank could see how worried Mandy was

119

becoming. 'He'll be back by the morning,' he said gently.

But Mandy wasn't so sure. 'There's something wrong, Frank,' she said. 'I just know it.'

Mandy knew her cats well. She'd had them for three years – since they were kittens, adopted from the same litter at a Cats Protection Adoption Centre. Neither cat had ever missed a mealtime before. They liked their routine. They liked each other. Just like all brothers, they had their squabbles, but every night they'd go to sleep, side by side in their basket, the best of friends.

After a sleepless night, Mandy got up early. There was still no sign of Felix. She fed Jasper, then went out to shout for him again.

'I'll check with the neighbours,' said Frank. 'Maybe he's got stuck inside one of their sheds.'

But he hadn't. Mandy and Frank searched for most of the day. Still they didn't find him. It was mid-afternoon when a builder working next door heard Mandy calling for Felix.

'Are you looking for a black and white cat?' he asked.

Mandy nodded. 'Have you seen him?'

The builder looked grim. 'There was a cat in a terrible state came out of that field yesterday afternoon. I think it had got snarled up in the combine harvester. I tried to catch it, but it was too distressed. It ran off. It was covered in blood. Look . . .' he said, pointing to one of the slabs, 'you can still see some of its blood on the stones.'

Mandy's stomach lurched. She *had* to find Felix.

Frank phoned their vet. Felix was microchipped; a tiny chip under the skin at the back of his neck had their contact details on it. If he was found by someone, and taken to the vet, they'd scan him, and know immediately whose cat he was. But no one had brought a badly injured cat in.

Then, after an agonizing few hours, a neighbour called. He'd spotted Felix, dragging himself hopelessly around the bottom of his garden.

When Mandy and Frank arrived, they could barely recognize him. His back right paw hung limply to the side. His tail was crushed and his fur was soaked through with blood. His eyes were glassy, unfocused, staring off into the distance. He kept trying to stand up, then falling back down again. He was shivering, and yet hot to touch.

They wrapped Felix in a towel and, as gently as they could, took him to the vet's.

'Can you cope with a cat with no tail and only three legs?'

Mandy and Frank had been waiting in reception for what seemed like hours, while the vet assessed Felix's injuries. Now he stood, solemn-faced, in front of them.

'If he's to have any chance of survival,' said the

vet, 'I'll have to remove his right back leg, and his tail.'

Mandy didn't hesitate. 'So long as you think it's fair on him,' she said, 'then we'll manage.'

'He's a young and healthy cat,' said the vet. 'If his internal organs aren't damaged, then I'll operate. But you should prepare yourself for the worst,' he said gently. 'His injuries are so severe, he may not make it.'

It was a difficult operation. The vet had known it would be. He'd set up his film camera to record it. If the cat survived, the film would be useful, to show student vets that sometimes the impossible *is* actually possible.

Eventually Felix was taken to the recovery room, where Mandy briefly saw him, still sleeping off the anaesthetic.

'If he lasts the night,' said the vet, 'he's got a chance.'

Felix *did* last the night and, though heavily

sedated, he recognised Mandy when she came to visit him the next day.

'He's a little fighter,' said the nurse who was caring for him. She stroked his head gently. 'He'll make it, I know he will.'

Mandy felt it too. Felix *would* survive. They were willing him to survive.

Remarkably, he recovered from the operation quickly. And by the end of the week, Mandy was able to take him home to recuperate. But the happy homecoming was short-lived. A few days later, Felix took a turn for the worst. His breathing was bad, and he seemed to be choking, unable to eat or drink. Mandy and Frank rushed him back to the vet's.

'It doesn't make sense,' said the vet, shaking his head. 'All the signs point to a tetanus infection, but that's extremely rare in cats.'

It was true. Tetanus – a highly dangerous

infection that causes muscle spasms, and breathing difficulties – is much more common in larger animals such as horses or pigs. Indeed, it was so rare, the vet's practice didn't have the medicine they needed to treat it. But the vet wasn't beaten.

'We'll send word to the horse hospital,' he said, 'and see if they can give us the medication we need. Somehow we'll have to scale down the dose, to suit a much smaller animal.'

It was another anxious wait. The medicine arrived from the horse hospital, but there was no guarantee it would work. Too big a dose would kill Felix; too small and he would die anyway, from tetanus. The effect of the illness was already so severe by this time that Felix had become paralysed from the neck down, unable to move at all.

Mandy and Frank sat watching the clock in the waiting room. 'Come on, Felix,' said Mandy to herself. 'I know you can do it.'

125

Bumble the Brave Kitten

Felix battled on. The nurse who was looking after him took great care, washing him gently, cleaning his whiskers with a cotton bud, and feeding him with a dropper. At lunchtimes, she took him out to the garden on a soft cushion, so he could smell the fresh air and feel the warm sun on his battered body. He had little fur left. They'd had to shave most of it off when they'd amputated his leg and tail. He looked a sorry state, and yet, there was still a spark in his eye. The nurse noticed it. And so did Mandy. She visited him daily, watching and hoping for signs he was recovering.

Three days later the feeling started to come back to his front paws. He could move them again, but his surviving back leg still hung limply.

'He must recover the use of that leg,' said the vet. 'He can manage fine with three legs – but not two. If that leg doesn't recover, he won't be able to stand up, and if he can't stand up, it wouldn't be fair to keep him alive.'

'Come on, Felix,' Mandy said softly, when she visited him each day. 'You can do it. You've come so far – just one more battle.'

Days turned to weeks, and his remaining back paw still wouldn't work. Felix dragged himself sadly around his pen at the vet's. The situation looked hopeless. And then . . . a phone call came.

'Is that Mandy? It's Debbie from the vet's.'

Mandy felt her chest tighten. She was at work, and hadn't been expecting a call.

'What's happened?' she said, trying to keep her voice steady. 'Is Felix OK?'

'He's walking!' said the nurse. 'His back leg has started working again, and he's managed to stand up and walk. He's going to be all right.'

After that Felix's recovery was fast. Being able to move again seemed to spur him on. Suddenly he was eating better. His sleek, beautiful fur was growing back. And within days, Mandy was finally able to take him home. But there was one final hurdle . . . Jasper.

In all the drama, Jasper had not been forgotten. But after weeks away from his brother, would he accept him home again?

'Cats can be funny,' warned the vet. 'Felix will smell different – he's been here with us so long, and he'll look and feel different to Jasper. It may take a while for them to settle back down together.'

But they needn't have worried. After only a day or so of cautious watching and waiting, the brothers were back to their rough-and-tumble wrestling best, squabbling over treats, fighting for cuddles, and then eventually flopping down to sleep, snuggled up beside one another, as usual.

Felix had beaten the odds. He might have lost

one or two of his nine lives along the way, but he'd fought back, becoming stronger as a result. With his three legs, he wasn't quite the mighty hunter he'd once been. And in truth, he now lolloped around the garden, more like a big bunny than a mini panther. But he was still able to do most of the things he'd done before. His balance wasn't so good – without a tail, he couldn't walk along fences any more, and jumping up on to things was difficult – but he could still run around, and play.

The vet had told Mandy that animals are more resilient and adaptable than humans. And as she watched him, from her kitchen window, hopping around the garden, she could see exactly what he meant. Felix found new ways to do everything he wanted to do. Even mouse-catching, though that took him a while to perfect. But it wasn't long before Mandy saw him padding back from the fields with a small mouse in his mouth – proud as punch!

Bumble the Brave Kitten

That was another strange thing. Felix still played in the field where his awful accident had happened. But even if she'd wanted to, Mandy wouldn't have been able to stop him.

Mandy was grateful for the skill and devotion of the vet and his nurse. Their courage and care had saved Felix's life. She was also understandably proud of Felix, and when she spotted an advert for a competition to find the country's bravest cats, she couldn't resist entering.

Of course he won – and was named Cats Protection's ultimate survivor champion! Felix became an international star. His picture appeared in cat magazines around the world. A television company came and filmed him for a programme about amazing animal operations, and loads of newspapers printed his story. Felix took it all in his stride. He wasn't one for the limelight – he was actually a rather shy cat, much preferring quieter times; cuddles with Mandy, Frank and Jasper.

It was a year or two after the accident, and Mandy was in her front garden, doing a spot of weeding. Felix was by her side, lolloping around the garden on his three legs, chasing a butterfly or rolling in the sunshine, when a small boy walked past with his mum.

'Excuse me,' he said. 'Are you the lady who owns the cat with the bits missing?'

Mandy smiled. She couldn't have put it better herself. 'I am,' she said proudly. 'I certainly am.'

Donna

There were four of them; bored teenagers, loud and intimidating. They were larking around, looking for targets; soft ones, easy to pick on. They'd already hurled abuse at an old man walking his dog. Then they spotted the black cat.

Small and painfully thin, she'd been straying around the estate for weeks. Someone said her owner had died, and the relatives had slung her out. But no one really knew, and they didn't much care. Stray cats were common enough. Several lived on the waste ground, scavenging for scraps, competing for food with a colony of feral cats who ruled the patch.

Donna

The tallest boy saw her first. He nudged his mate and nodded in the cat's direction. The other two soon caught on. The cat was oblivious; sniffing around a half-eaten bag of chips, the smell of the vinegar making her eyes water, but too hungry to care.

Then one of them picked up a stone, acting the big man in front of his mates. He aimed low. It missed the cat but she took off, racing across the waste ground to find cover. She hid behind an old sofa, dumped months ago – now charred and crumbling. But they followed her, bending to pick up more stones. As they approached, she ran off again, this time under a hail of stones. She raced down a back alley of terraced houses. But still they followed. More stones were thrown. Then one struck her on the side and another followed straight after, catching her on the head. Dazed, the cat stumbled, and then the boys surrounded her. One picked up an old tin of paint, left lying by a bin. Another held a petrol can.

Moments later there was a shout.

'You lot! What are you doing there?' It was a big angry voice. A man putting out his bins in the alleyway had heard the commotion. 'What are you doing there?' he growled again. He could see a small cat cowering at the boys' feet, her coat covered in paint. The man sniffed – he could smell petrol too. Then he spotted a lighter in one boy's hand. 'Get out of here, all of you!' he shouted at them. 'Before I call the police!'

The boys shouted abuse at the man, but they backed away. The cat took her chance, and escaped up the alley, instinctively searching for some-where high up, out of reach, where she would be safe. She saw a telegraph pole, and hauled herself up, her young claws digging into the old wood. Higher, higher she climbed until she reached the top. She stayed there then, her eyes shut, her breath shallow. And suddenly the street was quiet again.

Jill grimaced, then put the food dish down quickly, and withdrew her hand. She glanced briefly at the place where the cat had just bitten her, but she wasn't cross. Her eyes showed nothing but pity. 'Poor mite,' she said softly, carefully closing the pen door. She stayed for a few moments, ignoring the pain in her hand, and talked kindly to the cat, telling her it would all be all right . . . she really hoped it would.

The staff at the Cats Protection Adoption Centre in Belfast had seen a lot of mistreated animals in their time. But this was one of the worst. When the cat had finally come down from the pole, too weary to cling on any longer, the man with the big voice had scooped her gently into a box, covered her with a blanket and taken her to the vet. There they'd worked hard to remove the paint and petrol from her fur and checked her over for injuries. They were gentle and caring, but the cat shrank away from their touch, cowering and shaking. Although her physical injuries were minor, the mental scars ran deep.

As soon as she was signed off by the vet, Cats Protection stepped in to find her a home. It wouldn't be easy. Although she was young, barely a year old, Donna, as they named her, was now terrified of people. She shied away from everyone, attacking aggressively if she felt threatened in any way. The staff were sympathetic. They accepted the scratching and biting. They ignored the hissing and spitting. And they did their best to calm and reassure her, finding unusual ways to approach her – such as going towards her on their hands and knees, so they wouldn't tower over her threateningly. Their strategy worked, and she stopped attacking them as soon as they opened her pen. But she still didn't want to be touched, and progress in gaining her trust was slow. Donna was deeply troubled.

Then, a few months after she'd arrived, more misfortune found her.

Gramps McGinty spotted her as soon as she appeared in the exercise pen. He was a big cat, loud and friendly, who liked nothing better than a good-natured wrestle with the other cats in the home. But Donna wasn't interested. She didn't much like the exercise pen. It was a place where cats had space to jump, and climb, and run. It was also where they learned to mix with other cats – an essential skill, if their potential new family already had a cat at home. But Donna was too afraid to try.

Gramps followed her around the pen, batting her tail a few times. But Donna didn't want to play. Instead, she jumped on to the climbing frame to get away from him. But Gramps wasn't giving up. He followed her along the bars, batting her tail playfully again. Donna quickened her pace, and reached the top of the frame. Now there was nowhere else to go. She turned and gave Gramps a warning hiss, but her balance wasn't so good, and when Gramps gave her one final bat with his paw, she fell, landing badly.

Bel, one of the Adoption Centre staff, was close by. She heard Donna's cries and came quickly, finding her cowering on the ground, Gramps looking down innocently from above.

'It's OK, girl,' said Bel softly, trying not to scare Donna. But the cat shied away, her eyes closed.

Her hip was badly broken. In time it would heal, but it was a huge setback for Donna, who had already been through so much. She hated the treatment and attention she needed from the vet. And found it difficult to lie still while she mended. A dark cloud of misery seemed to have descended over her again, making her moods even blacker than before.

'Come on, Donna,' Jill and Bel and the other staff would will her. 'You're a fighter, don't give up now . . .'

But Donna was growing gloomier by the day. When her hip healed, she was left with a permanent stiffness, which made walking, let alone exercising, painful. As a result, she spent more and more time in her bed, reluctant to move, and began to put on weight. The staff tried to help – giving her a special diet and encouraging her to exercise – but Donna was slowly retreating into herself, becoming more and more miserable. It was as if she'd given up on life, and didn't want to be involved with anything or anyone any more.

The staff had to break the downward spiral Donna was plunging into. They took the first step, one beautiful sunny morning. Jill unfastened her pen. 'Come on, girl,' she said. 'You're free today, to wander around all by yourself.'

It was a new plan. In an effort to get Donna moving more, and to raise her spirits, they would let her out of her cat pen, to roam around the centre freely. They hoped it would give her more confidence.

At first Donna ignored the open door. But after a while, curiosity got the better of her, and she clambered unsteadily out of her pen, and began to explore. By the afternoon she had found somewhere, somewhere that would become her favourite place – the staffroom, where she curled up straight away in a quiet corner and slept peacefully. It was a strange choice for a cat who distrusted humans so much. But Donna had taken her first steps to regaining her confidence. And although she still hated to be touched, she had actually grown quite fond of the staff. She liked being around them. She liked their company, their warmth and gentle patience – and she was gradually starting to trust them more. It was this trust that led to a huge breakthrough.

It happened one afternoon, a few weeks later. Jill and Bel were in the staffroom. It had been a difficult day – lots of new arrivals; many troubled animals. They were chatting together, enjoying their break, when Donna suddenly got up from her basket, stretched the stiffness from her hip, and looked directly at them.

Bel nudged Jill. 'Look!' she whispered. Donna was slowly coming towards them. They held their breath, terrified they'd make a wrong move and frighten her.

Donna padded over, and with a confidence they hadn't realized she had, jumped up on to Jill's knee. Instinctively Jill started to stroke her. Then Bel nearly dropped her tea: Donna was purring! They had finally reached out to her!

Bumble the Brave Kitten

It had taken long months of patience to bring Donna so far, and yet she still had so much further to go. The staff at the centre never gave up on her. Many of them had developed a special fondness for the troubled cat. Noeleen, a newer member of staff, who had joined the centre long after Donna had arrived, immediately felt drawn to her – finding time to give her a few extra cuddles, and play with her. As a result of the attention she got, Donna's behaviour was improving. She still had her limits, and the staff knew when she'd had enough, but her confidence with them was growing.

She was still terrified of strangers though. And despite dozens of appeals in the newspapers, and on the Adoption Centre website, nobody came forward to take her on. In many ways it was understandable. On the few occasions anyone showed interest in her, Donna would cower away from them, or worse, lash out and bite or scratch them! It was frustrating for the staff. As much as *they* loved her, they were beginning to wonder if anyone else ever would.

Months turned to years, and still Donna had no home. Staff and volunteers came and went. As did cats and kittens – nearly 4,000 of them in the time Donna was there. Most cats at the centre were rehomed within months, but not Donna. She seemed destined to stay forever. She witnessed many changes at the centre – the whole site was rebuilt, almost around her, and a new rehoming wing was constructed. Donna watched it all with sad resignation. She'd given up even bothering to respond when potential adopters appeared. And they in turn passed by quickly. And then one day Donna's world changed. After nine long years in the centre – a lifetime for some cats – someone did come, and this time, they *didn't* pass by.

Pamela Gray had had a difficult year. A young accountant, with a busy life and a demanding job,

Bumble the Brave Kitten

she'd suddenly found herself living alone for the first time in her life. She had endured much sadness in recent months, and felt lonely and troubled. When a colleague suggested a cat might be good company, Pamela had at first dismissed the idea. Surely cats needed a big garden and someone at home all day. Pamela lived in a small flat, and worked long hours. But as her friend Linda told her, 'There's a cat for everyone . . .'

It was a Saturday afternoon, and Pamela was babysitting her little niece Emily. The girl was a smiley bundle of eighteen months, and Pamela adored her. The love was mutual; Emily saved all her best smiles for her favourite Auntie Pam! Pamela's friend Linda was visiting too, and they were discussing the cat idea, when Linda suddenly grabbed Pamela's arm. 'Get your coat! Come on, let's go down there right now, and have a look.'

Pamela hesitated, wondering whether the Adoption Centre was a good place to take

Emily – she was very young – but then again, Emily was a big part of her life, and whatever cat Pamela chose, *if* she decided to choose a cat at all, would have to get on with the little girl. Pamela fetched her coat and the three of them set off straight away.

But when they got there, Pamela briefly wondered if she'd made a mistake. She felt over-whelmed by the place. There were just so many beautiful cats, all desperate for a home.

Jill showed them around. She explained that some of them were house cats with special needs – disabled or sick; cats who preferred the indoor life. Suddenly Pamela's worry about not having a garden didn't seem to be an issue.

Linda and Emily walked ahead, looking closely in all the pens – Emily cooing at each new whiskery face. Pamela followed behind, finding it increasingly hard to walk past *any* of them. And then Linda stopped.

'Pam, come over here,' she said.

'Puss Puss,' cooed Emily. 'Lovely puss puss.'

It was Donna's pen.

Jill looked at the expression on Pamela's face. It wasn't one she'd seen before, not when people saw Donna . . . And Jill suddenly felt a twinge of hope. She told them Donna's story. It was hard to listen to. Pamela felt an immediate empathy with the cat. She tried not to cry. There was something so tragic, and yet compelling about Donna, the way she looked steadily into your eyes. Pamela felt drawn to her.

'She's had such a hard life,' Jill was explaining, 'that she takes a while to trust people, and sometimes she can nip or scratch if she feels threatened.'

But Emily wasn't listening. The wee girl had taken an immediate liking to the old black cat. And with the natural boldness of a toddler, she stepped forward, and stood, face to face, nose to nose, with Donna, cooing, 'Puss puss . . .'

Jill held her breath. How would Donna react? But amazingly, the cat didn't cower. She didn't shrink away. She didn't bite or scratch or back up defensively. She stayed exactly where she was, and let the little girl pet her. Jill sighed with relief. Pamela smiled. She knew then. She knew without any doubt that this was the cat for her.

Indeed, they seemed meant for each other. As Pamela filled in the adoption form later that afternoon, she noticed that the birth date the original vet had estimated for Donna was actually the same day as her birthday!

The Adoption Centre staff were sad to see Donna go. The place wouldn't be the same without her, but they were delighted too – Donna had beaten the odds and finally found a home.

And she settled quickly. Pamela had been prepared for trouble, but Donna was at ease immediately. The cloud of misery that had dogged her for so long seemed to have lifted the moment she arrived in the little flat. She padded around a few times, sniffing it, and finding her way, and then she climbed on to the sofa and got comfy!

When she went to bed that night, Pamela felt a light thud as Donna climbed up on the bed beside her, snuggling close. Later, she changed position, and settled above Pamela's head, as close as she could get. A bond had been made, never to be broken.

Within days, a new side to Donna emerged. It was a side the staff at the rehoming centre had seen glimpses of — a strangely affectionate nature that now knew no bounds. Donna loved cuddles on the sofa, purring happily on Pamela's knee, and covering her forehead with kisses. And she followed Pamela around, enjoying being close to her, watching her as she did the chores, seeming to listen with interest as Pamela chattered away (though Pamela later discovered she was deaf!). She was even happy to be around Pamela's family and friends. The scratching, biting, aggressive cat had gone – though she still occasionally got carried away when playing, as Pamela's poor granny found to her cost! But after everything she'd been through, Granny forgave the little nip delivered during a game.

Donna had finally found exactly what she'd been looking for all her life: a loving, caring home, with a very special lady. And Pamela in turn had found a little soul mate. A few weeks later, as she turned out the bedside light, Pamela reached up and gave the puss one last bedtime stroke. 'Goodnight, girl,' she said softly. 'I'm glad I finally found you – I'm just so sorry it took me so long.'

Bumble

The darkness closed in around the car. There were no street lights now, just an empty stretch of road, surrounded by fields — a few scattered houses, their lights pinpricks in the dark. A chill wind had picked up. It wasn't a night to be out.

The man driving slowed the car, checking carefully no one was around. He wasn't a brave man — he certainly didn't want anyone to see what he was about to do. He stopped the car, the engine still idling softly, then reached across and grabbed a small kitten, cowering in the footwell of the passenger seat. He grasped it by the scruff of its neck and held it up in front of him for a moment. It was the first time he'd actually looked at it properly. Small and dark, just ten weeks old. His daughter had brought it home. She'd named it Bumble. But he'd told her she couldn't keep it. He shook his head crossly, then opened the car door, and without hesitating, threw the kitten into the road. He didn't give it another glance. He revved the engine and, as the first raindrops began to fall, sped off into the night without a backward glance.

Bumble was dazed from the fall. Several times, more cars came, narrowly missing her as she drifted across the road. There were other noises too. Frightening sounds. An owl hunting. Foxes. Large rats, scurrying close by. But nothing lingered. Nothing stayed. The weather was too bad now. The rain fell heavily, soaking the small kitten, until she was shivering and cold to the bone. She dragged herself into the hedgerow. It felt safer there. She stayed a while — too frightened to sleep, too cold to move. She was confused and anxious.

As dawn broke, her throat parched, she drank raindrops from the wet grass. The road was busier now, and the sound of the traffic terrified her. A lorry thundered past, and she took fright, darting through the hedge to the other side, finding herself at the top of a gaping gully – flooded and muddy. She lost her balance, and scrambled downwards, falling, and rolling until she found her feet again. Her coat was covered in dirt now. She cried then. Mewed piteously. But there was no one to hear her. No one to scoop her up and rescue her. No one to warm her, feed her, reassure her. She stayed in the gully all day – it was too steep and too muddy for her to climb out.

By the afternoon, Bumble was weak and tired. Her energy had all been spent trying to escape. Now she clung to a tufted mound of grass and mud, a few feet from the icy floodwater below. And still the rain fell. She cried hopelessly. But soon she wouldn't have the energy left even for that.

Above her, by the roadside, a man waited for the bus. It was a remote spot, with few buses. His collar was turned up against the wind, his iPod humming quietly, the music relaxing him after a busy day's work in a nearby hotel kitchen. But as the track he was listening to ended, he heard the kitten's faint cries. He removed his earpiece and listened harder. It was definitely a cat. High-pitched and desolate. He scanned the fields; he peered down into the gully. But the kitten's mud-splattered coat blended too well to the ground cover, and he couldn't see her. He could still hear her though. *Where are you?* he thought, as he scanned the culvert again. The rain had eased off now, the mist had risen, but still he couldn't see her.

Just then his bus rumbled into view, but he kept searching, scanning the fields to catch sight of her.

Bumble the Brave Kitten

'Are you getting on?' The bus driver was tired – he wanted to be on his way. The man was torn. He wanted to help the kitten, but if he stayed, he'd have to wait another hour for the next bus. Reluctantly he climbed on board. But he didn't forget her. As soon as he got home he fetched the phone book, and dialled a number.

Len and Frances had been out in the garden when he rang. Volunteers for Cats Protection, they'd been rescuing and rehoming cats across Cumbria for years now. They'd saved hundreds. All shapes, all sizes. Different colours. Long-haired, short-haired. Feral cats and straying pets. Dozens of kittens. Many of them came to rest and recuperate in the couple's own home. They even had a couple of pens in their garden, where lost souls could find peace and comfort while the couple looked for good homes for them.

Len went to answer the phone, while Frances

finished up outside. When he reappeared moments later, she could tell from his face that another animal needed their help. They set off at once.

The best of the day had gone now. A light drizzle had begun to fall, and the afternoon had turned gloomy and dark once more. By the time they reached the bus stop, where the man had heard the kitten, the light was fading fast. But that didn't stop them.

They heard Bumble almost straight away; faint and weak, but still loud enough to attract their attention. The couple clambered over the hedge, and then caught their breath when they saw the muddy gully where Bumble was stuck. They called to her, hoping she'd come to them, but she was too weak to try. And she was frightened too. In the space of just a few hours, her world had been turned upside down. She'd gone from the warmth of the child's bedroom, curled up with her mum, being cuddled, fed, loved, to this . . .

Len tried to climb down to her. But the kitten was so scared she leaped away, dangerously close to the flooded waters. He pulled back, so as not to frighten her. He tried again, but got the same response. He sighed, and then returned to Frances, further up the bank. 'We'll have to trap her,' he said. 'She's too scared to let me help her.'

Frances nodded, but she was worried. Trapping the kitten would mean leaving a cage there overnight. Once she was caught in it, there would be no shelter for her, and the rain was falling heavily again.

Just then the kitten cried out, and they made one more desperate attempt to reach her. But anxious and panicking, Bumble still wouldn't let them get close enough. And the light had finally gone.

Reluctantly Len fetched the trap, and clambered down in the darkness, as far into the gully as he could, placing the trap close to a broken-down bramble hedge. Once she was in the trap, the gorse and brambles would provide the kitten with a bit of shelter from the biting wind. They put some food inside, then retreated. They'd return at first light.

It was a long night for the couple. Both found it difficult to sleep. And there was no need for the alarm clock to waken them. The first strands of daylight saw them dressed and ready, their car already packed.

Frances tried not to think what they might find in the trap. It had been a cold night, a very cold night. And the rain had fallen steadily. The tiny kitten had looked so weak when they'd last seen her. Another night in the gully might have been too much for her.

Dispiritingly, they heard no crying when they retraced their steps, clambering quickly over the hedge, and carefully down the muddy gully. But

Bumble the Brave Kitten

Frances could see at once that there was a shape in the trap.

Bumble was quiet now, her eyes closed. For one brief moment Len thought she might be dead. Then he noticed a faint tremble, along the kitten's tiny spine. Frances gathered her up in a soft dry towel. But the kitten didn't stir.

'We'll take her to the vet,' said Len softly. Both of them were aware it might be too late.

Neither said much as they drove off, though Frances wondered, as she always did at times like this, what led people to such cruelty. How could they abandon something so small? After decades spent caring for such animals, neither Len nor Frances had the answer – and they never got used to the dreadful neglect they'd witnessed.

The vet called them through at once.

'I can't see any injuries,' she said, turning the kitten gently in her hands. 'But the cold and wet has taken its toll. She's very weak, and needs warming up. Then we'll have a better idea.'

The vet gave the couple a heat lamp to borrow, with instructions to stand it above the kitten's pen, and let her warm up gradually. She waved away their thanks. She loved her job, and was touched by the little animal, resting peacefully now in Frances's arms. She respected the work the couple did, and admired them for it.

They followed her advice, and set up the lamp above a small kitten pen in their laundry room. They laid Bumble inside. Her eyes were still closed, and her breathing was weak. Both wondered whether she'd last much longer.

But the effect of the lamp was remarkable. Within an hour or so, the kitten became alert again, her eyes opening, her body twitching, and in another hour she was suddenly ravenously hungry. Frances had seen some miracles in her time, but even she was shocked at how quickly the kitten responded. The lamp seemed to jump-start her system. And soon she was eating again, drinking milk and enjoying a cuddle.

'She's obviously been loved by someone,' said Len, as he stroked the tiny kitten's head, and she purred back loudly. This was no feral kitten. From the way she accepted and enjoyed being held and stroked, she'd obviously been someone's pet. 'And she's litter trained,' he added.

But there was still one problem: what could they do about Bumble's coat? It was so caked in mud, it was impossible even to see her colour properly. Frances didn't want to put the kitten through any more trauma – she knew from experience how terrified cats could be when you tried to wash them. And anyway, the kitten had seen enough of water to last her a lifetime. But they had to get the mud off somehow. Then Frances suddenly remembered an old trick she'd used years ago.

Bumble

'Fetch a tin of sardines, Len,' she said.

Together they rubbed sardine oil into the little kitten's filthy coat. It was just the impetus she needed. She responded immediately to the strong smell of the fish oil – delicious to a hungry kitten – and started to lick herself clean.

Bumble, the brave kitten, had survived. For the next four weeks she stayed with Len and Frances, thriving under their care – growing stronger and less anxious with each day. But as much as they loved her, they knew she needed a home of her own. They wrote about her on the Cats Protection rehoming website. And almost immediately a young couple came forward to adopt her. Len and Frances vetted them carefully – Bumble was very precious to them and they didn't want her to end up in another bad situation – but the couple and the kitten suited one another perfectly.

Bumble the Brave Kitten

When they came to visit, they immediately fell in love with her, watching delightedly as she chased a small ball across the floor. Back and forward, never tiring with the game.

'Look at her,' said the lady, smiling down at the kitten, 'buzzing around that pen. She's like a little bumble bee.'

The kitten stopped playing at the word 'bumble' and looked up. It had been weeks since she'd heard her old name. Suddenly, in a flash, she remembered the girl who had named her. But it was just a fleeting memory, and the kitten soon returned to her game. She was looking forward now – not back – to a new future; a future that was bright and warm and stretched endlessly in front of her.

Cat Care

Cats Protection (CP) is the UK's leading feline welfare charity. Cats Protection has been helping cats since 1927 and each year we help more than 215,000 cats and kittens, giving them the chance of a better life.

CP volunteers and staff are motivated by a love of cats and a concern for their well-being. There are many reasons why cats come into our care, including:

When an elderly owner dies and there is no one else to care for kitty

When a cat has kittens and the owner can't look after them

Bumble the Brave Kitten

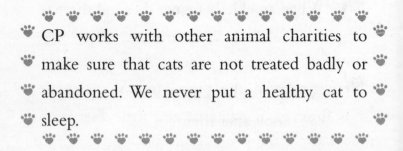

When cats are saved from unsafe places and cruelty

When couples separate, move house and can no longer keep their cat

When a cat is found wandering the streets and has no owner

Every cat is important to us and we make sure that they all see a vet for a check-up. Our adoption centres also vaccinate, neuter and microchip the cats.

CP works with other animal charities to make sure that cats are not treated badly or abandoned. We never put a healthy cat to sleep.

Rehoming

The most important part of Cats Protection's work is finding new homes for thousands of unwanted and abandoned cats and kittens every year. Cats come to us for many reasons and we spend lots of time making sure that each cat is ready for a new home and owner.

We always try to match the right cat with the right owner so that they'll have many happy years together. We believe there is a home for every cat!

Neutering

Neutering is the best way to stop more unwanted cats from coming into the world. Neutering is an operation which stops female cats from having kittens and male cats from becoming dads. It isn't cruel and actually helps your cat avoid fights and serious diseases.

One female cat can be responsible for around 20,000 family members in a lifetime. That's a lot of kittens and there just aren't enough homes in the UK to take them all in.

Did you know?

Cats are protected by law

In Scotland and Wales it is different, but in England all cats should:

Have a suitable place to live

Be given suitable food

Not suffer pain, injury or disease

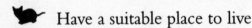

If people treat cats badly or steal a cat they may be arrested!

So you'd like to adopt a cat?

At Cats Protection we have over 7,000 cats and kittens in our care at any one time, all looking for the perfect home. If you're thinking about offering a home to a Cats Protection cat or kitten that's great news! There is a lot to think about, but we are here to make the adoption process as smooth as possible.

One of our main objectives is to find good homes for all the cats in our care. We want to make sure that the cat coming into your life is the right cat for you, your family, your lifestyle and your plans for the future.

When you adopt a cat you must be prepared to look after him for his whole life and take him to the vet at least once a year for a check-up and vaccination. There are other expenses such as feeding, litter and insurance, while you will also need to make sure your cat is looked after if you go on holiday.

There are several steps to adopting a cat from Cats Protection. First you should contact your local branch or adoption centre. You can find their details on our website www.cats.org.uk or by calling our Helpline on 03000 12 12 12 (Monday to Friday, 9 a.m.–5 p.m.).

Tell us about the kind of cat you are looking for and a little about yourself and your family. If you are visiting one of our adoption centres, you can also meet some of the cats looking for a home.

The next step is that someone from your local CP branch or adoption centre will visit you at home so they know which kind of cat would suit you and your family best.

After this visit you will get to meet some of the cats that are waiting to be rehomed. You can have a chat with the CP staff and volunteers about the cats' different characters.

Once you've chosen your cat you'll be told when you'll be able to collect him or her. Then it's just a matter of welcoming your new member of the family home!

If you have any questions after taking your cat home, please give the branch or adoption centre a call – we're here to help! Our National Helpline 03000 12 12 12 is also here to help you (Monday to Friday, 9 a.m.–5 p.m.).

Bumble the Brave Kitten

Cats make a house a home

When you take a cat home they will need:

Some toys to play with

A place for food and water

Somewhere nice to sleep

A scratching post

Somewhere to hide

Something they can climb on to sit and watch what is happening

A litter tray so that they can go to the toilet

Caring for your cat

Caring for a cat is a big responsibility and one that the whole family can share. Below are the key things that every young person should know about caring for their cat.

Regular vet checks

It is important that a cat sees a vet at least once a year for a physical check-up – teeth, ears, eyes, heart, etc. – booster vaccinations and deflea/deworm treatments. If you are at all concerned about your cat's health or behaviour you should see your vet as soon as possible.

Vaccinations

All cats should be vaccinated against the following diseases: feline infectious enteritis

(FIE), feline leukaemia virus (FeLV) and cat flu. All these can kill cats if they become infected, so it is important to protect your pet.

Feeding

A good diet is very important to keep your cat healthy. Choose quality tinned or dried cat food and always have a bowl of fresh water out. Cats are carnivores and cannot survive on a vegetarian diet.

Neutering

Neutering helps cats become happier and healthier pets. A neutered male is less likely to wander far from home and get into fights. A female cat that has been neutered will not have any more kittens, which is good, because there aren't enough homes for all the kittens in the UK as it is! A kitten should be neutered between four and six months of age, your vet will advise you on exactly when.

Fascinating fact

Microchips give cats a better chance of being found if they go missing: the cat owner's address is stored on the chip and a scanner can reveal who the cat belongs to.

Puzzles and Games

Cat riddle

As I was going to St Ives
I met a man with seven wives.
Each wife had seven sacks,
Each sack had seven cats,
Each cat had seven kits.
Kits, cats, sacks, wives,
How many were going to St Ives?

Answer: one – only me. I met them on the way!

Jokes

What do cats like to eat
for breakfast?

Mice Krispies

What do you call a cat with
eight legs that likes to swim?

An octopuss

Why do cats make terrible
storytellers?

They only have one tail

Why don't cats play card
games in the jungle?

*Because there are too many
cheetahs*

What do you call a cat that has
eaten too much duck?

A duck-filled fatty puss!

178

Puzzles and Games

Did you hear about the cat that drank three bowls of water?

He set a new lap record!

What is a cat's favourite Shakespeare quote?

Tabby or not tabby!

How do cats end a fight?

They hiss and make up!

True or false?
1. Cats sweat through their ears
2. An adult male cat is called a tom
3. Cats have more bones than humans

Answers: 1. False – cats sweat through their paws; 2. True; 3. True

Bumble the Brave Kitten

Quiz

Put your thinking cap on for our feline quiz and see how much you *really* know about cats . . .

1. The musical *Cats* is based on a book by whom?
a) Charles Dickens
b) William Shakespeare
c) T. S. Eliot

2. How long does a cat's pregnancy last?
a) Nine days
b) Nine weeks
c) Nine months

3. When was the cartoon *Tom and Jerry* first made?
a) 1939

Puzzles and Games

b) 1954

c) 1973

4. How fast can a domestic cat run?

a) Up to 10 mph

b) Up to 30 mph

c) Up to 50 mph

5. How many hours each day – on average – does a cat spend sleeping?

a) Three hours

b) Eight hours

c) Sixteen hours

6. Which term is used to describe a fear of cats?

a) Ophidiophobia

b) Ailurophobia

c) Arachnophobia

Answers: 1. c; 2. b; 3. a; 4. b; 5. c; 6. b

For more
cool cat facts, games and downloads
see the Cats for kids section of the
new Cats Protection website at
www.cats.org.uk/cats-for-kids

Acknowledgements

Many thanks to the staff, volunteers and friends of the Cats Protection for their help with this book, especially Lucy Holmes and Matt Vincent.

And a special thanks to the families and friends of the unforgettable cats whose stories are shared in this book:

Tizer Inspector Roy Sloane of the British Transport Police and his family, Judith, Ben and Jake

Stewie Kevan Owen and the staff at the Nottingham CP, and David, Rachel, Jacob and Ruby Gregory

Speedy Joan and Christine Payne and family

Noah Julia, Scott, Kirsty and James Malloch, and Stuart Webster

Munchie Vet nurse Kersty Ellis

Mr Ginge Mick Harrison and Sarah Forsyth, and Alex Downing, Claire Bennett and the elephant keepers at Colchester Zoo

Marmite Lindsey, Huw and Ruby Davies

Felix Mandy and Frank Parsall

Donna Pamela Gray, Jill Taylor, Bel Livingstone, Noeleen McCabe and the staff of the Belfast CP Adoption Centre

Bumble Frances and Len Morton, and Paula and Brett Johnson

A selected list of titles available from Macmillan Children's Books

The prices shown below are correct at the time of going to press. However, Macmillan Publishers reserves the right to show new retail prices on covers, which may differ from those previously advertised.

Anna Wilson

KITTEN KABOODLE	978-0-330-50771-4	£4.99
KITTEN SMITTEN	978-0-330-50772-1	£4.99
KITTEN CUPID	978-0-330-51832-1	£5.99
PUPPY LOVE	978-0-330-45289-2	£4.99
PUP IDOL	978-0-330-45290-8	£5.99
PUPPY POWER	978-0-330-45291-5	£4.99

Chosen by Anna Wilson

FAIRY STORIES	978-0-330-43823-0	£4.99
PRINCESS STORIES	978-0-330-43797-4	£4.99

All Pan Macmillan titles can be ordered from our website, www.panmacmillan.com, or from your local bookshop and are also available by post from:

Bookpost, PO Box 29, Douglas, Isle of Man IM99 1BQ

Credit cards accepted. For details:
Telephone: 01624 677237
Fax: 01624 670923
Email: bookshop@enterprise.net
www.bookpost.co.uk

Free postage and packing in the United Kingdom